AF352553

Playful Texts and the Emergent Reader

Playful Texts and the Emergent Reader

Developing Metalinguistic Awareness

Anne Plummer

Sheffield, UK   Bristol, CT

Published by Equinox Publishing Ltd.

UK: Office 415, The Workstation, 15 Paternoster Row, Sheffield S1 2BX
USA: ISD, 70 Enterprise Drive, Bristol, CT 06010
www.equinoxpub.com

First published 2016

© Anne Plummer 2016

All rights reserved. No part of this publication may be reproduced or transmitted in any form or by any means, electronic or mechanical, including photocopying, recording or any information storage or retrieval system, without prior permission in writing from the publishers.

ISBN: 978-1-78179-118-9 (hardback)

A catalogue record for this book is available from the British Library.

Library of Congress Cataloging-in-Publication Data

Plummer, Anne (Teacher)
Playful texts and the emergent reader: developing metalinguistic
awareness / Anne Plummer.
pages cm
Includes bibliographical references and index.
ISBN 978-1-78179-118-9 (hb)
1. Language awareness in children. 2. Plays on words. 3. Language
acquisition--Age factors. 4. Children--Language. I. Title.
P118.3.P58 2015
401'.4--dc23
        2015010605

Typeset by JS Typesetting Ltd, Porthcawl, Mid Glamorgan
Printed and bound in Great Britain by Lightning Source UK Ltd., Milton Keynes
and in the USA by Lightning Source Inc., La Vergne, TN

Contents

Figures

Acknowledgements

My sincere thanks to Janet Joyce, Val Hall, Geoff Williams, Ruth Lewin, Dipika Shrestha, Evan Johnstone, Judie Cross, Ellen Fiedler, Elizabeth Miles, Robyn Kemmis, Rita Proweller, Noela Symonds, Helen Clemens, Ruth Callaghan, Maria Gray, Sandra Patterson, Vivian Baruch, Zachary Chavez and Greg Newby (Project Gutenberg) for their generous assistance, support and advice while I was writing this book.

I would also like to express my thanks for permission to reproduce material from: *The Amazing Maurice and His Educated Rodents* text copyright © 2001 by Terry and Lyn Pratchett. Illustrations copyright © 2001 David Wyatt. Published by Corgi/Random House Children's Books. Reprinted by permission of The Random House Group Limited. In the United States and Canada, *The Amazing Maurice and His Educated Rodents* text copyright © 2001 by Terry and Lyn Pratchett. Illustrations copyright © 2001 David Wyatt. Published by HarperCollins Publishers. Used by permission of HarperCollins Publishers; *Anno's Peekaboo* by Mitsumasa Anno. Copyright © 1987 by Kuso-Kobo. Used by permission of Philomel Books, a division of Penguin Group (USA) LLC; *The Annotated Alice: The Definitive Edition* edited by Martin Gardner (Allen Lane 2000, Penguin Books 2001). Copyright © Martin Gardner, 1960, 1970, 1988, 2000, 2001. Reproduced by permission of Penguin Books Ltd. In North America, *The Annotated Alice: The Definitive Edition* edited by Martin Gardner. Copyright © 2000, 1990, 1988, 1960 by Martin Gardner. Used by permission of W. W. Norton & Company, Inc; *Black and White* by David Macaulay. Copyright © 1990 by David Macaulay. Reprinted by permission of Houghton Mifflin Harcourt Publishing Company. All rights reserved; *The Book about Moomin, Mymble and Little My* text and illustrations copyright © Tove Jansson 1952. English translation by Sophie Hannah, 2001. Text and illustration used by permission of Schildts and Söderströms, English translation used by permission of Sort of Books; *The Book That Jack Wrote* by Jon Scieszka, illustrated by Daniel Adel. Text copyright © 1994 by Jon Scieszka. Illustrations copyright

© 1994 by Daniel Adel. Used by permission of Viking Penguin, a division of Penguin Group (USA) LLC; *Child's Talk: Learning to Use Language* copyright © 1983 by Jerome Bruner. Used by permission of W. W. Norton & Company, Inc.; *The Development of Play* copyright © 1987, 1993 David Cohen. Published by Routledge. Used by permission of Taylor & Francis Books (UK); *Duck! Rabbit!* © 2009 by Amy Krouse Rosenthal. Illustrated by Tom Lichtenheld. Used with permission of Chronicle Books LLC, San Francisco. Visit www.chroniclebooks.com; 'First graders interpret Wiesner's *The Three Pigs*' by Lawrence R. Sipe in *Postmodern Picturebooks: Play, Parody, and Self-Referentiality* edited by Lawrence R. Sipe and Sylvia Pantaleo. Copyright © 2008 Taylor & Francis. Published by Routledge. Used by permission of Taylor & Francis Group LLC; 'The framework of "Tell me" questions' in *Tell Me (Children, Reading and Talk) with The Reading Environment* copyright © 1991, 1993, 2011 Aidan Chambers. Used by permission of The Thimble Press; *Harold and the Purple Crayon* © 1955 by Crockett Johnson. Copyright renewed 1983 by Ruth Krauss. Published by HarperCollins Publishers. Used by permission of HarperCollins Publishers; *How Texts Teach What Readers Learn* by Margaret Meek. Copyright © 1988 Margaret Meek. Used by permission of The Thimble Press; 'Helping teachers explore multimodal texts' by Michele Anstey and Geoff Bull in *Curriculum Leadership* (now *Curriculum and Leadership Journal*) 8(16), 4 June 2010. Copyright © 2010 Michele Anstey and Geoff Bull. Used by permission of the authors and the *Curriculum and Leadership Journal* www.curriculum.edu.au/leader; '"How could that be?": Reading Banyai's *Zoom* and *Re-Zoom*' by Sylvia Pantaleo in *Language Arts*, 84(3), January 2007, pages 222–233. Copyright © 2007 by the National Council of Teachers of English. Used by permission of the U.S. National Council of Teachers of English; *I Will Not Ever Never Eat a Tomato* by Lauren Child. Text and illustrations copyright © Lauren Child 2000. First published in the UK by Orchard Books, an imprint of Hachette Children's Books, 338 Euston Road, London NW1 3BH; *It's a Book* © 2010. By Lane Smith. Reprinted by permission of Roaring Book Press. All rights reserved; *The Jolly Pocket Postman* by Janet and Allan Ahlberg (Heinemann 1995). Copyright © Janet and Allan Ahlberg 1995. Reproduced by permission of Penguin Books Ltd. In the United States, *The Jolly Pocket Postman* by Janet and Allan Ahlberg. Copyright © Janet and Allan Ahlberg 1995. By permission of Little, Brown and Company. All rights reserved; *Meow Ruff: A Story in Concrete Poems* by Joyce Sidman. Text copyright © 2006 by Joyce Sidman. Reprinted by permission of Houghton Mifflin Harcourt Publishing

Company. All rights reserved; *My Heart Is Like a Zoo* copyright © 2010 by Michael Hall. Published by Greenwillow Books. Used by permission of HarperCollins Publishers; *Not a Stick* text and illustrations copyright © Antoinette Portis 2008. Published by HarperCollins Children's Books. Used by permission of HarperCollins Publishers; in the United States, its territories and dependencies, Canada and the Philippines, *The Mouse and His Child* by Russell Hoban. Scholastic Inc/Arthur A. Levine Books. Copyright © 1967 by Russell Hoban, copyright © renewed 1965. Used by permission; *The Phantom Tollbooth* by Norton Juster, Reprinted by permission of HarperCollins Publishers Ltd © 1961 Norton Juster. In the United States, its territories and possessions, and in the Republic of the Philippines, *The Phantom Tollbooth* by Norton Juster, text copyright © 1961, copyright renewed 1989 by Norton Juster. Used by permission of Random House Children's Books, a division of Random House LLC. All rights reserved; *The Pencil* written by Allan Ahlberg, illustrated by Bruce Ingman. Text copyright © 2008 Allan Ahlberg. Illustrations copyright © 2008 Bruce Ingman. Reproduced by permission of Walker Books Ltd, London SE11 5HJ www.walker.co.uk; *The People in the Playground* copyright © Iona Opie 1993. Published by Oxford University Press. Used by permission of the author; 'Picture book learning and teaching strategy' by Lesley Reece, The Literature Centre, Fremantle, Western Australia. Used by permission of the author; 'The reader in the book' in *Booktalk: Occasional Writing on Literature and Children* copyright © Aidan Chambers 1985, 1995. First published by The Bodley Head. Latest edition: The Thimble Press, 2001. Used by permission of The Thimble Press; *Reading Contemporary Picturebooks: Picturing Text* copyright © 2001 David Lewis. Published by Routledge. Used by permission of Taylor & Francis Books (UK); *The Red Book* by Barbara Lehman. Copyright © 2004 by Barbara Lehman. Reprinted by permission of Houghton Mifflin Harcourt Publishing Company. All rights reserved; 'The role of story: learning to read in a special education class' by Geoffrey Williams and David Jack in *Revaluing Troubled Readers*. Program in Language and Literacy, Occasional Paper no. 15, 12–39. Copyright © The University of Arizona College of Education, 1986. Used with permission of The University of Arizona College of Education; *Steps to an Ecology of Mind* copyright © 1979 by The Estate of Gregory Bateson. Published by The University of Chicago Press, 2000. Used by permission of The University of Chicago Press; *The Stinky Cheese Man and Other Fairly Stupid Tales* by Jon Scieszka, illustrated by Lane Smith. Text copyright © 1992 by Jon Scieszka. Illustrations copyright © 1992 by Lane Smith. Used by permission of Viking Penguin, a division of Penguin Group (USA) LLC; *Swallows and Amazons* copyright © Arthur Ransome, 1930. First published by Jonathan Cape, 1930. Published by Red Fox – Random House, 2010. Used by permission of The Arthur Ransome Literary Estate. In the United States, *Swallows and Amazons* by Arthur Ransome. Reprinted with permission of David R. Godine, Publisher, Inc. Copyright © 1986 Arthur Ransome; *The Three Pigs* by David Wiesner. Copyright © 2001 by David Wiesner. Reprinted by permission of Clarion Books, an imprint of Houghton Mifflin Harcourt Publishing Company. All rights reserved; *Through the Magic Mirror* by Anthony Browne. Illustration copyright © 1976, 2000 Anthony Browne. Reproduced by permission of Walker Books Ltd, London SE11 5HJ, www.walker.co.uk; '*Voices in the Park*, voices in the classroom: Readers responding to postmodern picture books' by Frank Serafini in *Reading Research and Instruction* Spring 2005, 44(3). Copyright © 1982–2005 The H. W. Wilson Company. All rights reserved. Used by permission of Taylor & Francis Group and the author; 'Ways of telling: From writer to reader: An author reads himself' in *Booktalk: Occasional Writing on Literature and Children* Copyright © Aidan Chambers 1985, 1995. First published by The Bodley Head. Latest edition: The Thimble Press, 2001. Used by permission of The Thimble Press; *Who's Afraid of the Big Bad Book?* by Lauren Child. Copyright © Lauren Child 2002. First published in the UK by Hodder Children's, an imprint of Hachette Children's Books, 338 Euston Road, London NW1 3BH; *The Worm Book* copyright © Janet and Allan Ahlberg, 1979. Reproduced by permission of Penguin Books Ltd; *Zoom* by Istvan Banyai. Copyright © 1995 by Istvan Banyai. Used by permission of Viking Penguin, a division of Penguin Group (USA) LLC.

Every effort has been made to trace copyright holders to request permission for the use of material. The publishers will be glad to make suitable arrangements with any copyright holders whom it has not been possible to contact.

1 Introduction

> Dear Reader, pleased to meet you;
> Welcome to this book.
> Enclosed you'll find a useful lens.
> It's in here – take a look!
> Read on, read on!
> Read in and out!
> Read up and down and *round*.
> (This story hurtles through the air;
> It burrows underground.)
> And use your lens to peep and spy.
> There's more in here than meets the eye.
> Janet and Allan Ahlberg, *The Jolly Pocket Postman*[1]

1.1 Playful texts?

This book is about playful picturebooks and novels. It is my conviction that reading playful texts has significant benefits for young readers, especially in the area of metalinguistic awareness – the ability to identify and talk about the properties of language that is so critically important in the development of language and literacy skills.

The case for playful texts rests on a number of key concepts. Most importantly, what qualifies as 'playful'? Alphabet puzzles, nonsense verse and fractured fairy tales? I would say these are definitely playful. Comic stories with jokes and tongue twisters? Talking animals and toys-come-to-life? Perhaps, but not always. Pop-up books, codes and ciphers? Yes, if they fulfill the criteria for textual playfulness. Let me explain.

The best books for children have always been texts with 'deep reading secrets'[2] – texts that are imaginative in scope and innovative in language, illustration and design; texts that reveal more with each reading. These are some of the qualities which characterize the finest works of children's literature, but they do not necessarily produce a playful text. To be considered playful, a text must play on words and/or images in the same way that children play in games of make believe, transforming the everyday world of common sense meaning into a self-reflexive playworld which works to disclose, and subvert, the rules which sustain it.

Playful texts subvert the conventions of storytelling and narrative fiction. They specialize in multiple storylines, unreliable narrators, language play, parodies and nonsensical lists. We can therefore say that playful texts are essentially metafictive texts: texts which comment, reflexively, on the process of fiction writing. These are books which tell us what books are. In the following chapters I show how playful texts encourage young readers to reflect upon, and question, the meaning-making procedures of narrative fiction. It is this process which enhances development in areas such as metalinguistic awareness, metacognition and perspective taking.

While there has been a vast amount of research on the role of make-believe play in children's cognitive and linguistic development, and the links between reading and play have been studied from different perspectives, the specific function of playful texts in literary reading has yet to be explored.

What is it about engagement with playful narrative which seems to enable many young readers to tolerate uncertainty and explore different ways of looking at the world? To take risks as readers and ask 'what if'? In my view, the key is to be found in the imaginative, world-creating function of make-believe play and in its metacommunicative nature[3] – the fact that play 'is not just about play but is also a message about itself (a metamessage), being both of the world and not of the world.'[4] When players signify that 'this is play,' they engage in a process of recontextualization accompanied by a shift from 'as-is' to 'what-if' thinking. They create an imaginary world, framed by its own set of rules, which is both divorced from and contingent upon the 'real world.' As long as they abide by the rules of the game, players are free, within their playframes, to be themselves and other than themselves at the same time. It is this freedom, I argue, that enables players to adopt an interrogative point of view as far as the making of meaning is concerned.

Playful texts behave in precisely this way. Conveying the message 'this is fiction, this is play,' these self-conscious texts make room for developing readers, inviting them to become co-players and co-producers.

Taking their cues from the metacommunicative dimension of make-believe play, the texts employ transparent strategies which serve simultaneously to draw attention to the making of textual meaning and to disclose the processes by which those meanings are made. There is nothing covert about this procedure. As I will demonstrate, playful fictions work by revealing the narrative practices on which they rely. Strategies typically include play with narrative codes and conventions (including the interplay of printed word and visual image), play with levels of narration and framing devices, and play with language itself – extending the meaning of words and creating alternative patterns of signification.

My investigation of textual playfulness begins with children's wordplay and literary nonsense. I have chosen to focus on nonsense because it is the most audacious of textual playforms, shameless in the way it subverts linguistic rules, especially the rules of semantics, in its creation of fictional worlds. I then turn to multimodal texts and novels for young readers, paying particular attention to those which overturn narrative conventions, highlight the intertextual nature of fiction, and engage in extended play with nonsense, metaphor and other figurative forms of expression.

These books demand a high degree of inference making from young readers but players gain confidence as they read in partnership with the text, and the rewards are great. As we will see, these are texts which invite developing readers to discover new ways of looking at the world; to take on challenges, solve puzzles and acknowledge other perspectives, learning more about the ways other minds mean in the process.

1.2 Postmodernism and new literacies

In the past 20 years there has been a proliferation of picturebooks with characteristics which children's book critics have been eager to define as 'postmodern.' The postmodernist worldview rejects orthodox, hierarchical structures, embraces multiplicity, and is more interested in questions than answers. Postmodern literature aims for transparency. It draws attention to its fictional status and seeks to involve the reader in the creative process in as many ways as possible. As a result, postmodern texts scorn linear narratives and employ various metafictive techniques.

There is no doubt that these tendencies are evident in many contemporary children's books, particularly picturebooks. Discerning an emerging trend, critics have identified a new literary genre: 'the postmodern picturebook.' This form of picturebook is distinguished by the following features:

- Explicit intertextuality (texts alluding to other texts).
- Metafictive effects and self-referentiality (highlighting the fact that the text is an artefact).
- Playfulness. Parody and subversion of literary genres and conventions.
- Multiple perspectives accompanied by a high degree of ambiguity and a low degree of resolution. Stories tend to be open ended.
- Collapsing distinctions between:
  - popular and high culture;
  - author, narrator and reader; and
  - written word and the visual image. Word and image are utterly interdependent. The picture book has become a picturebook.
- Undermining the traditional distinction between the story and the real world.[5]

The first three points are closely linked since intertextuality involves playful allusion to other texts and forms of discourse, and play/playfulness is always metacommunicative. The reference to playfulness, however, is more problematic. Studies of postmodern picturebooks invariably refer to 'play' and 'playfulness' but they rarely say what they mean by these terms.[6] In this study I take the opposite approach. While the picturebooks and novels discussed in the following chapters exhibit most if not all of the 'postmodern' qualities listed above, they are not necessarily postmodern. In fact, many of them date from the nineteenth and early twentieth centuries – well before the postmodernist era. My concern is with *playful* texts – metafictive, interactive, frame-breaking, boundary-blurring, intertextual, intermedial, playful texts – not merely postmodern ones.

The play of the text is not, of course, confined to the printed page. Children growing up in the digital age enter into the new literacies of hypertext, messaging and electronic games. These young readers are familiar with multiple, overlapping texts and deeply embedded images. They encounter narrative complexity online, in television programs and in films. Within the digital environment, readers/players feel that they are in control of their digital world, and they learn to negotiate multimodal (linguistic, visual, audio, kinaesthetic and spatial) patterns of meaning.[7] While it's impossible to overestimate the impact of e-technology on reading (and play), I have chosen to focus on printed texts in this study. With so many textual opportunities on offer, it seems to me to be more important than ever to make the very best books available to children. Lane Smith makes the case well:

'It's a book.' [said Monkey]
'Look.'
   'Arrrrrrrrr,'
   nodded Long John Silver, 'we're in agreement then?'
   He unsheathed his broad cutlass laughing a maniacal laugh,
   'Ha! Ha! Ha!'
   Jim was petrified.
   The end was upon him.
   Then in the distance, a ship!
   A wide smile played across the lad's face.
'Too many letters.' [said Jackass]
'I'll fix it.'
   LJS: rrr! K? lol!
   JIM: :(! :)[8]

1.3 Chapter outline

I explore the origins of pretend play in Chapter 2, charting its emergence in infancy as an intersubjective phenomenon. I also discuss the ways caregivers support children's understanding of pretence, guiding the transition from 'as-is' to hypothetical, 'as-if' thinking, and providing the foundations for fully fledged make-believe play.

Acknowledging the work of play theorists such as Gregory Bateson, Catherine Garvey, Brian Sutton-Smith and Angeline S. Lillard, I examine the defining features of make-believe play (the characteristics which account for its metacommunicative and paradoxical nature), and discuss the ways those characteristics enable players to transform the everyday world of 'the *here and now*, the *you and me*, and the *this or that*,'[9] and create new worlds of meaning, playworlds where things both are and are not what they seem to be.

I point out that make-believe play always involves role playing: imagining oneself in the role of another, and exercising the role-taking (or perspective-taking) skills needed to effect that transformation. I reflect on the view that make-believe perspective taking provides children with the tools they need to construct a theory of other minds, and I briefly examine some of the research in this fascinating area of cognitive science.

Finally, I draw attention to the links between playful, what-if thinking and mental reflexivity, the mind's ability to think about its own mental processes. This allows me to introduce two quintessentially reflexive play-forms: language play and nonsense.

In Chapter 3, I describe language play as a metalinguistic game which manipulates the rules of linguistic discourse. Following Chukovsky, I place language play at the center of parent–child interaction, and demonstrate that it is crucial for language learning. I highlight the importance of rhythm and rhyme (nursery rhymes, nonsense verses, finger games, lullabies and jingles) in the development of children's language play, and show how purely phonological play makes way for more complex forms of play with structure and semantics.

Increasingly elaborate language games (tested and refined in the school playground) allow for the bending and breaking of conventional linguistic rules, a process which is essential when it comes to metalinguistic aware-ness. It is in this context that I discuss the incorrigible forms so loved by children: the riddles and jokes, puns and conundrums which play with the syntax, sound, shape and meaning of words in countless ways.

This leads me to the subject of nonsense, the most radical form of lin-guistic play. Unlike puns and metaphors, playforms which transform one world of meaning into another, nonsense is meant to be taken literally. Focusing on literary nonsense texts by Lewis Carroll and Edward Lear, I show how nonsense interrogates the rules of language to produce texts which abound in meaning but signify nothing at all. Drawing on the insights of critics such as Susan Stewart, I also discuss some of the meaning-making strategies which characterize literary nonsense. I will refer to these again, in various guises, as I pursue the subject of playful texts. Before that, I need to clarify my theoretical position with respect to literary reading.

In Chapter 4, I define literary reading as a playful, interactive process, learned in collaboration with more experienced readers and pursued in di-alogue with the text itself. The basis for my argument is to be found in the work of Margaret Meek, Wolfgang Iser and Jerome Bruner, scholars who characterize reading as a playful transaction between reader and text made all the more meaningful when texts leave gaps and pose puzzles which en-gage the reader's imagination in the task of working things out for him or herself.

I highlight the similarities between reading and play, and contend that reading is a partnership which transforms the reader and the text. To en-gage in that process, I argue, readers need to be aware of the multiple in-fluences at work in a narrative – the intricate patterning of narrative voices within the text, and the many intertexts with which the text engages and within which it is situated. It at this point that I acknowledge my debt to Mikhail Bakhtin, the great scholar of dialogicality and intertextuality.

I conclude the chapter by noting that the first texts children encounter are likely to be picturebooks, multimodal texts which require readers to negotiate two different sense-making systems: words and images. I also point out that playful picturebooks can *show* and *tell* quite different stories, transforming early reading sessions into exciting adventures in making meaning.

In Chapter 5, I turn to the subject of textual playfulness and examine a selection of playful texts in some detail. I set the scene by tracing the development of ludic elements in books written specifically for children from the eighteenth century onwards, looking at toy books and novelties, and the many books in which toys come alive. I refer to the host of books which feature mazes and puzzles, discuss texts for young readers which re-enact childhood games of various kinds, and pay my respects to classic texts which celebrate make-believe play such as the *Swallows and Amazons* series and *The Story of the Treasure Seekers*.

Acknowledging that all of these texts represent play in one form or another, I stress that they are not necessarily 'playful texts' in the sense that I use the term in this book. I designate as 'playful' those self-reflexive narratives which clearly signal 'this is fiction, this is make-believe,' and invite young readers to engage in the transformative play of the text.

While reluctant to categorize such profoundly subversive texts, I take a strategic approach to textual analysis, focusing on the following metafictive techniques.

- **Narrative frame breaking**. Playful texts like to defy genres and disrupt narrative conventions in various ways. Techniques include retelling traditional stories from unusual perspectives, destabilizing the levels of narration that shape the fictional world, presenting multiple (and occasionally contradictory) storylines, and facilitating co-authorship by readers, characters and narrators. Texts discussed include *The Three Pigs, Bear Hunt, The Pencil, Black and White, The Mysteries of Harris Burdick, A Pack of Lies* and *Clockwork*.

  Playful texts may also feature embedded images and stories within stories which reflect, challenge or extend the primary narrative. Outstanding examples reviewed in the chapter include *Flotsam, Zoom* and *The Red Book*.
- **Mirror imagery**: *mises en abyme*. The *mise en abyme*, the mirror-like reproduction of a written text or visual image within itself, is

one of the hallmarks of playful metafiction. To illustrate the process in action, I focus on several multimodal texts and on Russell Hoban's novel, *The Mouse and His Child*, where, in a process of 'ungoing into going and back again,' a dazzling *mise en abyme* weaves in and out of the text, shaping it and replicating its themes in miniature.

- **Language play and visual games**. Well versed in the rules of linguistic discourse and pictorial composition, playful texts delight in visual jokes and wordplay. My survey encompasses make-believe alphabets (*On Beyond Zebra, Chicka Chicka Boom Boom, The Disappearing Alphabet* and *Eye Spy*), invented languages (*Mr Wuffles!*), play with the eccentricities of syntax and semantics (*The Phantom Tollbooth*), contextual learning (*Baloney (Henry P.)*), and sustained play with world-creating figurative language and illustrations (*Anno's Peekaboo, My Heart is Like a Zoo* and *I Will Not Ever Never Eat a Tomato*).
- **Verbal and visual nonsense**. By taking a preposterous proposition as far as it can logically go, nonsense texts interrogate conventional systems of classification and test the limits of discourse. They enjoy surrealist imagery, and tend to be obsessed with inventories and lists. My selections include *The Worm Book, The Mouse and His Child, Bamboozled* and *The Lost Thing*.
- **Intertextuality**. While all of the playful texts included in this book have dialogical elements, some are more explicitly intertextual than others. I focus on texts which flaunt their intertextuality – jubilant, ingenious texts such as *The Jolly Pocket Postman, I Was a Rat! … or The Scarlet Slippers, Voices in the Park* and *The Amazing Maurice and His Educated Rodents*.

In the final chapter, Chapter 6, I offer a number of practical scaffolding strategies developed for parents and teachers by experts in literary reading. These include simple techniques which can be used during shared-reading sessions to build inference-making skills, and more complex strategies to support critical thinking in older children, encouraging them to pay attention to narrative processes and share their observations with others. Recognizing that multimodal texts can also be an excellent resource for introducing literary theory to secondary students, I present a model for the secondary classroom together with recommended teaching materials.

I also present a number of case studies, spanning several decades, of children interacting with playful texts discussed in this book. My aim has been to present a wide range of studies conducted with children of different ages and in different contexts. These include David Lewis's conversations with young children reading *Time to Get Out of the Bath, Shirley* in a London primary school; Williams and Jack's collaborative reading of *Bear Hunt* with inexperienced readers in outer-suburban Sydney; and, in the United States, reading circle discussions with six year olds encountering Wiesner's *The Three Pigs* for the first time; literature workshops with eight to 11 year olds reading *Voices in The Park*; and analysis of responses by fifth grade children engaging with the wordless text, *Zoom*. These studies show young children building visual literacy and metalinguistic awareness, negotiating complex sense-making procedures, and reveling in narrative play. Here we see textual playfulness in action.

Notes

1 Janet and Allan Ahlberg, *The Jolly Pocket Postman* (London: William Heinemann, 1995; New York: Little, Brown and Company, 1995).

2 Margaret Meek's phrase, used to describe John Burningham's picturebooks in her influential study: *How Texts Teach What Readers Learn* (Stroud, UK: The Thimble Press, 1988), 15.

3 As identified by Gregory Bateson in his definitive paper 'The message "This is play,"' reprinted in *Child's Play*, ed. R. E. Herron and Brian Sutton Smith (New York: John Wiley and Sons, 1971), 261–266.

4 Brian Sutton-Smith, *The Ambiguity of Play* (Cambridge, MA: Harvard University Press, 1997), 139.

5 This list is based on the work of Lawrence R. Sipe and Caroline E. McGuire as cited by Sylvia Pantaleo and Lawrence R. Sipe, 'Introduction: postmodernism and picturebooks,' in *Postmodern Picturebooks: Play, Parody and Self-Referentiality*, eds. Lawrence R. Sipe and Sylvia Pantaleo (New York: Routledge, 2008), 3.

6 This is not to underestimate the work of scholars such as David Lewis who write on picturebooks and play. Lewis considers 'the special relationship that exists between picturebooks, the child reader and the concept of play' and discusses the ways in which 'playful picturebooks ... adopt game-like disguises, break rules and subvert conventions' in *Reading Contemporary Picturebooks: Picturing Text* (London and New York: Routledge/Falmer, 2001), 76–86. He also argues that 'picturebook makers recognize [the] need for play in children and frequently respond with forms of text that are game-like and playful. Play is what children do, not because they are in a state of innocence, but because they are

perpetually learning, perpetually becoming, and the best picturebook makers are their allies in this.' (p. 81). I endorse this position, but go further, developing a definition of 'playful' which takes account of the metacommunicative nature of children's make-believe play.

7   The implications for teaching and learning are explored at www.newliteracies. com.au.

8   Lane Smith, *It's a Book* (New York: Roaring Brook Press, 2010; London: Macmillan Children's Books, 2012).

9   Catherine Garvey, *Play*, rev. ed. (Cambridge, MA: Harvard University Press, 1990), 82.

2 Make-believe play and the making of meaning

'We ought to sign it in our blood,' she said, 'but pencil will do.'
John took the paper and signed, 'John Walker, Master.'
Nancy signed it, 'Nancy Blackett, Amazon Pirate.'
The two captains shook hands.
Peggy said, 'Well, it's peace today, anyhow.'

Arthur Ransome, *Swallows and Amazons*[1]

2.1 The development of pretend play

Pretence is one of the great mysteries of human cognition. All primates play, but, as far as we know, only humans pretend. We begin to pretend in the first year of life, learning to do so in interaction with other minds. This is not surprising in itself: sense-making is an interactive process regardless of the form it takes. Pretend play, however, is unique in two critical respects.

First, pretend play/make-believe (I use the terms interchangeably in this book) requires players to deliberately misrepresent reality. This is an astonishing achievement, given our impulse, as infants, to understand the world around us. And yet we see very young children, assisted by their mothers or caregivers, developing the ability to sustain two distinctly different versions of reality.

Second, the projection of an alternative, make-believe world onto the real world is accompanied by a form of speculative, 'as-if' thinking. While fully fledged symbolic play – the ability to create imaginatively realized counterfactual worlds – does not emerge until much later, infants of 12–24 months of age readily participate in pretend play sessions scripted and directed by their mothers. The process looks something like this:

Hey, be careful with that stick

Figure 1 From *Not a Stick* by Antoinette Portis

It's not a stick

Figure 2 From *Not a Stick* by Antoinette Portis

The fact that very young children can recognize that 'this is play', and can engage in abstract as-if thinking, is certainly remarkable. To understand exactly what is entailed, we need to examine the development of pretend play in early childhood.

As stated, sense-making is an interactive, dialogical process from the beginning. Soon after birth and well before entry to the first language, infants engage in protoconversations, communicating with their caregivers by means of eye contact and facial expressions, touch, gestures and vocalizations.[2] In the first few weeks of life infants are capable of sharing attention with their mothers, addressing them and recognizing that they are being addressed.[3] These interactive phenomena represent the first systematic acts of meaning on the part of a newborn child.

The mode of interaction between caregiver and child is inherently playful. For the first nine months or so, the adult sets the scene by establishing a communicational environment, or frame, where a range of expressive attributes can come into play. Here, the two engage in a series of dramatic performances which can be seen as paradigms for subsequent ludic behavior.

As described by Brian Sutton-Smith, these interactive routines may take one or more of the following forms:

- exchange routines, where the mother mimics the baby, establishing a clear connection between action and response. This prompts the baby, in turn, to study her[4] mother and repeat her earlier sound or action;
- central-person routines, where one person takes the leading role and the other responds;
- unison routines, generally involving shared vocalization of sounds; and
- mock-contest routines, the antecedents of games with sides, rules, and outcomes that determine who is the winner.[5]

Everything about these mock-theatrical routines supports the belief that the baby is capable of 'reciprocal communication.'[6] Mothers emphasize the rules of conversational turn taking and maximize the opportunities for playful verbal interaction. Child-directed speech (baby talk) during the performance typically involves rhythmical expression, heightened pitch and varied intonation, accompanied by stylized gestures and facial expressions – all of which are designed to capture attention and elicit response. The inventive use of nonsense and incorporation of simple games such as 'Round and round the garden' and 'peekaboo' also serve to introduce language play into the equation at a very early stage, establishing the foundations for the subsequent development of symbolic, pretend play.[7]

Around the age of nine months, when most infants are able to crawl and gain new perspectives on the world and everything in it, an important development occurs in the form of a 'deliberate, self-conscious and reciprocal sharing of focus with another.'[8] More complex interactive features such as turn taking (as opposed to the formalized exchange routines noted above) and the convergence of the gaze onto the same object expand the range of the protoconversations considerably.[9] As they learn the rules of participation by interacting with the adults around them, babies begin to respond to games of peekaboo and to initiate simple games of their own.

Peekaboo is a perennial favorite. Since so many texts adopt the peekaboo theme (a quick literature search will reveal scores of examples), it is worth considering the fundamental principles of the game and some of the reasons for its lasting appeal.

Anno's Peekaboo illustrates the basic procedure:

Figure 3 From *Anno's Peekaboo* by Mitsumasa Anno

Regardless of how it is played (as people-peekaboo or peekaboo with toys and other objects, as plain peekaboo or a variant like 'Ride a cock horse'), peekaboo delights in the paradoxes which underlie our earliest perceptions of self:

- Now you see me
  - Now you don't
- Here I am
  - And now I'm not

Studies conducted by Bruner, Cazden and others characterize peek-aboo as a social exchange game based on the physical activities of hiding and finding.[10] Player interaction tends to follow a predictable structure in which the adult initially enacts the entire script. The child then assumes an increasingly active role, eventually taking on all the parts first spoken/acted by the adult. In time their roles become completely reversible.[11]

Each round of the game rests on the same sequence of moves, though certain variations (changes in who or what is hidden, and in what is used to conceal the hidden person or object) are permitted. To play the game successfully, participants must respect the rules and cooperate in their execution. As will become evident in my detailed discussion of *Anno's Peekaboo* in Chapter 5, the rules can themselves become a resource for play, a move calling for even greater cooperation between players.

There are several additional points to be made about the rules of peek-aboo and the ease with which infants generally learn them. First, peekaboo 'is a version of the Freudian *fort/da* game, a game which is implicated in the ability to understand object permanence and to construct an absent other.'[12] Seen in this way, peekaboo clearly has a valuable role to play in the lives of infants who are just beginning to make sense of the world outside themselves.

Second, and this is a related point, playing by the rules of peekaboo gives children an opportunity to explore the boundary between reality and make believe, with all of the benefits that that may entail: 'We have never in our sample of peekaboo games seen a child exhibit the sort of separation pattern noted ... when the mother *really* leaves the scene.'[13]

Third, as mentioned briefly earlier, the rules of the game require players to adopt play roles, take turns, anticipate another's actions and reactions, and generally manage interactions in a collaborative manner. Supportive adults assist in this process, eventually encouraging the child to assume an active role in initiating and maintaining the game.[14]

Fourth, peekaboo games often provide the first occasion for the child's systematic use of language with an adult.[15] The collaborative nature of the process and the emphasis on exchange of meaning between players is particularly striking. In the following account, Jerome Bruner refers to a game of peekaboo played with a jack-in-the-box clown:

> By [1.2] Jonathan could participate as agent or as experiencer. But now
> some negotiation was needed to decide who was to be the agent. He
> preferred the active role but did not monopolize it. He played it rather
> well; first ejecting the clown from its cone while vocalizing his variant of
> *boo!* (*ooo!*), then approximating his mother's *all gone* (*a ga*) while stuffing
> the clown back into its cone. Finally, he imitated his mother's *peekaboo*
> with *pick* as he yanked the clown out again and stuffed it back. When his
> mother served as agent, Jonathan gestured (raising his arm) and vocalized
> (*ah*) to signal the reappearance of the clown ... Now together, facing and
> smiling at each other, Jonathan and his mother called out *boo!* ... Roles had
> become completely interchangeable. The game itself had also provided a
> structured format to which Jonathan's burgeoning linguistic powers could
> be applied.[16]

Finally, the peekaboo theme of hiding and finding, disguise and recognition, is the foundation upon which riddling and other forms of enigmatic
language play are constructed. Like peekaboo, the riddle 'is designed to
make the listener become lost in the wrong track of associations, until he
finds his way back into a new, yet shared, path of associations with the
riddler.'[17] Both are dialogical forms and both entail transformations in the
shared process of making meaning.

As noted, caregivers deliberately simplify their games to make it possible for the child to be the leader. Analysis of joint picturebook reading at
this early stage confirms that mother-infant interaction has a decidedly dialogical structure with its own reciprocal rules and feedback mechanisms.[18]
It is this emerging emphasis on turn taking, on give-and-take and the grad-
ual accommodation of another's perspective, that points to the making and
communication of meaning as an intersubjective process.

By 12 months of age, most children are well on the way to becoming
conscious players. Piaget observed the process in action,[19] but saw it as a
transitory, solitary activity. Vygotsky[20] and more recent play theorists have
argued that pretend play is a profoundly social phenomenon – an extension
of the interactive bond between parent and child.

Numerous studies over the past 25 years have revealed that most pretend play by very young children is in fact initiated by mothers or caregivers. As documented by Angeline S. Lillard and her colleagues, adults tend
to re-enact real events and everyday behaviors in these play sessions, often
making use of props (real objects or replicas) in their performances.[21] This
is play of the 'as-if' variety: pretending to eat, to drink, to get dressed, and
to go to sleep. While the here and now is transformed to a certain extent,

and players are definitely aware that they are playing, this is a prototypic play phase. Things are still firmly in the realm of the possible.

Parents scaffold their children's understanding of pretence in various ways. First of all, as directors of the play session, they ensure that the signal 'this is play, let's pretend' is as transparent as possible. The procedure tends to be as follows:

- catching the child's eye to establish joint attention;
- initiating an action (pouring 'water' from a real jug or tasting 'soup' from a real bowl); and
- signaling by smiling that 'this is play,' and is not to be taken seriously.[22]

In most cases young children get the message and respond accordingly. During the play session mothers use various techniques to strengthen the playworld and sustain play. They tend to move differently, assuming a faster pace than normal, although some actions, such as mock eating and drinking, may be slow and exaggerated. Adults also vary their tone of voice, elevating pitch and generally speaking more loudly than they would outside the playframe.

We have noted how early interactions between parent and child are infused with verbal games and sound making. Make-believe play offers further opportunities for language development, and it is fascinating to see how caregivers support those opportunities in pretend situations. There is a lot of talking during pretend play, but the emphasis is always on real objects rather than the absent, hypothetical ones. This approach seems to serve two purposes. It reinforces, by repetition, the meaning of familiar words, and foregrounds any new words that are introduced. It is interesting to note that adults are careful not to overuse the words 'I'm pretending.' They are rarely used more than once per play session, and frequently not at all.[23]

With practice, children's pretend play skills become increasingly sophisticated. By 24 months of age most children can engage in pretend object substitution (using one object 'as if' it were another) and by 36 months, purely imaginary objects come into play. There is also considerable evidence to suggest that young children engaging in pretend play are, by this age, capable not only of relating to another person and the impersonal world of objects but also to 'the *other person's* relatedness towards the world and towards themselves.'[24] This playful form of intersubjectivity may be the earliest manifestation of the human ability to make inferences about other minds and to predict behavior accordingly. I will return to this intriguing subject in my discussion of role play, later in this chapter.

From the age of three, children's acts of pretence become increasingly complex. Closely scripted mother-infant play begins to give way to pretend play with siblings and peers, and we can detect significant developments such as the pretend animation of objects, the creation of imaginary characters, the assumption of distinctive play roles, and the emergence of social play forms.

2.2 Make-believe play and perspective taking

As we have seen, the ability to convey the message 'this is play' emerges early in infancy. Adults initiate the first pretend play sessions, which usually involve everyday objects or miniature toys. In pretend play young children reveal that they are capable of thinking hypothetically. They can think of one object as if it were another; and they can think of one object as two things at once.[25] The process is exemplified in *Duck! Rabbit!*, an ingenious picturebook for young readers.

Figure 4 From *Duck! Rabbit!* by Amy Krouse Rosenthal and Tom Lichtenheld

These representational abilities become even more sophisticated as older players move from hypothetical, as-if thinking to imaginative play of the 'what-if' variety. What-if behavior transforms reality. It enables players to change one object into another, create imaginary worlds, try out different personae, and negotiate different roles.[26] It is now time to consider the attributes of make-believe role play which support these accomplishments.

While it is pursued voluntarily and strictly for its own sake, make-believe role play[27] is governed by definite rules and is framed by distinct boundaries in time and space. It is symbolic (in as much as it stands for something beyond itself)[28] and it is transformative, as we have noted. Furthermore, it is capable of renewing itself in constant repetition.

Taken individually, each of these attributes is quite plausible. But the composite picture is more problematic. Can something be utterly free and strictly rule-governed? Can the play space, with its clearly delineated temporal and spatial borders, allow for uncertainty? Is it inconsistent to claim that something essentially intrinsic, something pursued for its own sake, can serve simultaneously to mirror and transform external reality? These difficulties can only be satisfactorily resolved if one accepts the paradoxical nature of play. Gregory Bateson expressed it this way:

> Expanded, the statement 'This is play' looks something like this: 'These actions in which we now engage do not denote what those actions *for which they stand* would denote.' ... We face then two peculiarities of play: (a) that the messages or signals exchanged in play are in a certain sense untrue and not meant; and (b) that that which is denoted by these signals is nonexistent.[29]

From this perspective, the message 'this is play' must involve a logical act of negation – a suspension of disbelief, during which the normal way of framing classes and relations is altered and new contextual frames are created which promote novel ways both of interpreting and relating to the world outside oneself.

Play is a metacommunicative activity. It can only occur if the participants are capable of exchanging information about the communication of meaning. When players signify that 'this is play' they are clearly conveying that from that point until further notice things should be interpreted as existing in an ambiguous, paradoxical realm where meaning both is and is not what it appears to be.[30] Regardless of the form the play signal takes, its expression depends on the ability to conceive of and communicate something which exists and does not exist at the same time. Indeed, it is the process of contextual reframing – the process of recontextualization involved in moving in and out of the playworld – which allows children to interrogate the procedures by which meaning is made in the first place.[31] After all, one must know the rules of the game in order to manipulate them.

Within their playframes children are free to exercise their imaginations and create new worlds of meaning for their own purposes. As a minimum, the make-believe world always involves transformation and always demands some degree of role taking. I will touch on the issue of transformation before turning to the critical subject of role play and perspective taking.

Make-believe play entails the 'transformation of the *here and now*, the *you and me*, and the *this or that*, along with any potential for action that these components may have.'[32] At least four types of transformation are possible: self-transformation; other-transformation; situation transformation; and object transformation or substitution.[33] As will be explained in my discussion of nonsense and other playful narrative forms, ludic transformations tend to take the form of repeated reversals, substitutions, exaggeration, fragmentation and reconstitution of self, other and event.[34]

In order to effect and sustain these transformations, young players must assume an orientation capable of tolerating contradiction and acknowledging when things both are and are not what they seem to be. In the case of collaborative role play, this process also involves the coordination of meaning between players.[35]

Role playing, according to George Herbert Mead, involves 'being another to one's self.'[36] Strictly speaking, role playing, the overt process where a child observes herself in the role of another, needs to be distinguished from the covert role taking (or perspective taking) that accompanies role-playing behavior. In other words, the role-playing child can be said to be 'organizing the attitudes and perspectives of the others whose role responses are being produced.'[37]

Role-taking skills develop progressively, especially in social play. With the refinement of these skills, the child continues to add new complications to her role-taking repertoire. Building on the intersubjective abilities established in infancy, she becomes increasingly adept at imagining (and enacting) other points of view and at stepping outside herself to view the self from other perspectives.

The implications of perspective taking in make-believe play have yet to be fully explored. There is support for the view that pretend play provides children with tools they need to construct a theory of other minds and may be crucial to 'the very human process of discovering that other people have ideas, hopes and beliefs – and that these can be influenced and manipulated.'[38] This is a fascinating but contentious area of inquiry. I can only touch on the key issues here: readers who wish to pursue the subject in more detail should refer to the notes.[39]

Theory of mind and reflexive thinking

By the age of five, most children will have developed a theory of mind which enables them to read other people's mental states. This critical ability allows the child to:

- infer that other people have their own beliefs, emotions, intentions and desires;
- understand that these may not coincide with one's own point of view; and
- discern the causal links that exist between events, mental states and behavior.[40]

Theory of mind skills are also implicated in the ability to distinguish between appearance and reality, and to appreciate the distinction between doing and thinking.[41]

The evidence seems to suggest that children demonstrate more advanced theory of mind skills in pretend play situations than they do in other contexts. There is considerable theoretical debate about this issue. As noted earlier, very young children can handle complex cognitive tasks in pretend play sessions and they seem to show enhanced levels of understanding in the playsphere. While children's 'mind-reading' skills certainly do appear to be highly developed in early make-believe play, there is a possibility that 'pretend play somehow makes children appear to be more advanced than they really are, and hence pretend play is in a sense "fool's gold."'[42]

There is less ambiguity about the situation when it comes to sociodramatic play. In order to engage in make-believe role play, three year olds must be able to predict behaviors and negotiate other points of view. They also need to be able to communicate with other players in and out of the playframe. Researchers investigating the links between role play and theory of mind frequently comment on the importance of language in this process, noting that role play gives children the opportunity to exercise developing language skills in new and imaginative ways. Dialogue between players needs to be sufficiently rich and flexible to establish and maintain the playframe, assign and negotiate roles, make plans and communicate feelings. Children who enjoy interactive social dialogue with their families and friends clearly have an advantage here, as do children surrounded by evocative, playful language and stories with their own fictional worlds. All of these resources may be considered to be partners in the accelerated development of theory of mind.

While we still have much to learn about the relationship between pretend play and theory of mind, we can definitely say that children who engage in metacommunicative play framing, who are capable of stepping outside themselves to ask what if and to take on other roles, demonstrating an ability to transform their immediate environment and their social relationships in the process, are actively involved in making meaning and reading other minds.

Within the liminal realm of what if, anything seems possible. And so it is, but only on strictly circumscribed terms and conditions. Ultimately, what-if thinking is completely dependent on the everyday world of common-sense meaning. Kornei Chukovsky, who highlighted the significance of imaginative thought and nonsensical word games in early childhood, stressed this point when he pointed out that in 'topsy-turvies' (make-believe nonsense rhymes which reverse the usual order and relationship of things) the pretence is enjoyed to the extent that there is awareness of the self-deception and a conscious recognition of play as play.[43] Seen from this meta-perspective, what-if thinking is essentially a matter of mental reflexivity – of the mind's ability to think about its own mental processes. As Chukovsy observed, one of the best ways to study reflexive thinking is through the prism of language play and nonsense. It is time to consider these phenomena in more detail.

Notes

1   Arthur Ransome, *Swallows and Amazons* (London: Red Fox, 2010), 121; (Boston, MA: David R. Godine, Publisher, 2013), 111–112.

2   See, particularly, C. Trevarthen, 'Sharing making sense: intersubjectivity and the making of an infant's meaning,' in *Language Topics: Essays in Honour of Michael Halliday*, ed. R. Steele and T. Threadgold, vol. 1 (Amsterdam: Benjamins, 1987), 177–199 and Trevarthen, 'The self born in intersubjectivity: the psychology of an infant communicating,' in *The Perceived Self: Ecological and Interpersonal Sources of Self-Knowledge*, ed. Ulric Neisser (Cambridge: Cambridge University Press, 1993), 121–173.

3 M. A. K. Halliday and Christian Matthiessen, *Construing Experience Through Meaning: A Language Based Approach to Cognition* (London: Cassell, 1999), 611.

4 I have alternated personal pronouns throughout this book.

5 Based on Brian Sutton-Smith, 'Epilogue: play as performance', in *Play and Learning*, ed. Brian Sutton-Smith (New York: Gardner Press, 1979), 300.

6 Catherine E. Snow, 'The development of conversation between mothers and babies', in *Child Language: A Reader*, ed. Margery B. Franklin and Sybil B. Barten (Oxford: Oxford University Press, 1988), 35.

7 L. R. Goldman, *Child's Play: Myth, Mimesis and Make-Believe* (Oxford: Berg, 1998), 13. Goldman points out that baby talk is built on 'the metaphorical underpinnings' of social pretence: 'i.e. the occurrence of renaming, the nominal predication of one identity onto another.' As we will see, mothers also engage in explicit pretend play scenarios with their infant children.

8 C. Trevarthen and P. Hubley, 'Secondary intersubjectivity: confidence, confiding, and acts of meaning in the first year', in *Action, Gesture, and Symbol*, ed. A. Lock (London: Academic Press, 1978), cited in Ragnar Rommetveit, 'Language acquisition as increasing linguistic structuring of experience and symbolic behaviour control', in James V. Wertsch, *Culture, Communication and Cognition: Vygotskian Perspectives* (Cambridge: Cambridge University Press, 1985), 188.

9 Rommetveit, 'Language acquisition', 188, 194.

10 See, particularly, Jerome S. Bruner, *Child's Talk: Learning to Use Language* (New York: W. W. Norton and Co., 1983); Jerome S. Bruner and V. Sherwood, 'Peekaboo and the learning of rule structures', in *Play – Its Role in Development and Evolution*, 277–285; Courtney B. Cazden, 'Peekaboo as an instructional model: Discourse development at home and at school', in *The Sociogenesis of Language and Human Contact*, ed. Bruce Bain (New York: Plenum Press, 1983, 40–42; and David Cohen, *The Development of Play* (London: Routledge, 1993), 92, 100–103, 188–190.

11 Cazden, 'Peekaboo as an instructional model', 40.

12 John Stephens, *Language and Ideology in Children's Fiction* (London: Longman, 1992), 169.

13 Bruner and Sherwood, 'Peekaboo and the learning of rule structures', 284.

14 Cohen, *The Development of Play*, 104: 'Round the age of nine months, most mothers give their children the chance to become active rather than passive. They ease them into the role of starting the game ... [making] the structure of peekaboo more simple so the [the child can] start off mastering its simplest form. This device helps shape the behaviour of the child. At six months, he can't participate in any [structured] game because he doesn't have either the attention or discipline to wait ... Six months later, he is master of the rules of

this particular game, knowing where to start, when to stop, when to take his turn and how to react to various predictable cues. It is a major achievement.'

15 Bruner, *Child's Talk*, 45.

16 Ibid., 54–55.

17 This relationship is discussed by Shlomith Cohen in 'Connecting through riddles, or the riddle of connecting' in *Untying the Knot: On Riddles and Other Enigmatic Modes*, eds. Galit Hasan-Rokem and David Shulman (New York: Oxford University Press, 1996), 303.

18 Anat Ninio and Jerome Bruner, 'The achievement and antecedents of labelling,' *Journal of Child Language* 5(1) (1978), 1–15.

19 Jean Piaget, *Play, Dreams and Imitation in Childhood*, trans. C. Gattegno and F. M. Hodgson (New York: W. W. Norton and Co., 1962), especially 96–97.

20 See, for example, L. S. Vygotsky's *Mind in Society: The Development of Higher Psychological Processes*, eds. M. Cole, V. John-Steiner, S. Scribner and E. Souberman (Cambridge, MA: Harvard University Press, 1978).

21 My discussion of mother–infant pretend play is based substantially on Angeline S. Lillard, 'Mother–child fantasy play,' in *The Oxford Handbook of the Development of Play*, ed. Anthony D. Pellegrini (New York: Oxford University Press, 2011), 284–295.

22 Ibid., 293.

23 Ibid., 289.

24 Peter R. Hobson, 'Perceiving attitudes, conceiving minds,' in *Children's Early Understanding of Mind: Origins and Development*, ed. Charlie Lewis and Peter Mitchell (Hove: Lawrence Erlbaum, 1994), 75.

25 Angeline S. Lillard, 'Mother–child fantasy play,' in Pellegrini, *Oxford Handbook of the Development of Play*, 349.

26 Inge Bretherton, 'Representing the social world in symbolic play: reality and fantasy,' in (ed.) Inge Bretherton, *Symbolic Play: The Development of Social Understanding* (Orlando, FL: Academic Press, 1984), 3–41.

27 The research on play in the last 60 years is extensive. Useful overviews can be found in Catherine Garvey's *Play*, rev. ed. (Cambridge, MA: Harvard University Press, 1990); J. L. Singer and D. Singer, *The House Of Make Believe* (Cambridge, MA: Cambridge University Press, 1990); Brian Sutton-Smith's *The Ambiguity of Play* (Cambridge, MA: Harvard University Press, 1997); and Pellegrini, *Oxford Handbook of the Development of Play*.

For specialist studies of language play, see Mary Sanches and Barbara Kirshenblatt-Gimblett, 'Children's traditional speech play and child language,' in *Speech Play: Research and Resources for Studying Linguistic Creativity*, ed. Barbara Kirshenblatt-Gimblett (Philadelphia, PA: University of Pennsylvania Press, 1976), 65–110, and Guy Cook, *Language Play, Language Learning* (Oxford: Oxford University Press, 2000).

Readers may also wish to refer to the influential works of Johan Huizinga: *Homo Ludens: A Study of the Play Element in Culture* (Boston, MA: Beacon Press, 1955) and Roger Caillois: *Man, Play and Games*, trans. Meyer Barash (New York: Free Press of Glencoe, 1961). Caillois defines four categories of play: *agon* (competitive games), *alea* (games of chance), *mimicry* (make-believe play) and *ilinx* (play involving vertigo, giddiness and loss of physical equilibrium). While my study focuses on make-believe play, there is an intriguing connection to be made between *ilinx* and certain heady forms of language play.

28 Goldman, *Child's Play*, 43: 'As its etymological root of *prae-tendere* (Latin: "stretch forth") betrays, pretending involves the imposition of one representation over or "in front of" another.'

29 Gregory Bateson, *Steps to an Ecology of Mind: Collected Essays in Anthropology, Psychiatry, Evolution and Epistemology* (Chicago, IL: University of Chicago Press, 2000), 180, 183.

30 Ibid., 183. Also see Sutton-Smith, *The Ambiguity of Play*, 1, 196.

31 Susan Stewart, *Nonsense: Aspects of Intertextuality in Folklore and Literature* (Baltimore, MD: Johns Hopkins University Press, 1978), 21–37.

32 Garvey, *Play*, 82.

33 Marilyn Guttman and Carl H. Frederiksen, 'Preschool children's narratives: linking story comprehension, production and play discourse,' in *Play, Language and Stories: The Development of Children's Literate Behaviour*, ed. Lee Galda and Anthony D. Pellegrini (Norwood, NJ: Ablex Publishing Corp, 1985), 112.

34 For an exhaustive study of the narrative devices used to effect ludic transformations in literary texts, see Stewart's *Nonsense*. On the general subject of self-other transformations in the playspace, see D. W. Winnicott, *Playing and Reality* (London: Routledge, 1971), 1–25.

35 Holly Giffin, 'The coordination of meaning in the creation of a shared make-believe reality,' in Bretherton, *Symbolic Play*, 73–100.

36 G. H. Mead, *Mind, Self and Society* (Chicago, IL: University of Chicago Press, 1934), 213, quoted in Greta Fein, 'The self-building potential of pretend play or "I got a fish, all by myself,"' in *Child's Play: Developmental and Applied*, ed. Thomas D. Yawkey and Anthony D. Pellegrini (Hillsdale, NJ: Lawrence Erlbaum Associates, 1984), 126.

37 Fein, 'The self-building potential of pretend play,' 126.

38 Cohen, *The Development of Play*, 191.

39 Representative works include Simon Baron-Cohen, 'Theory of mind in normal development and autism,' *Prisme* 34 (2001), 174–183. Retrieved on 28 June 2014 from www.autism-community.com/wp-content/uploads/2010/11/TOM-in-TD-and-ASD.pdf; J. H. Flavell, 'The development of children's knowledge about the mind: from cognitive connections to mental representations,' in *Developing Theories of Mind*, ed. J. W. Astington, P. L. Harris, and D. R. Olson

(New York: Cambridge University Press, 1988); and H. M. Wellman, *The Child's Theory of Mind* (Cambridge MA: Bradford/MIT Press, 1990).

On the specific subject of pretend play and theory of mind, see: Doris Bergen, 'The role of pretend play in children's cognitive development' in the *Journal of Early Childhood Research and Practice* 4(1) (2002) retrieved on 28 June 2014 from http://ecrp.uiuc.edu/v4n1/bergen.html; Robert D. Kavanaugh, 'Origins and consequences of social pretend play,' in *The Oxford Handbook of the Development of Play*, op. cit., 296–307; and Angeline S. Lillard, 'Pretend play skills and the child's theory of mind' in *Child Development* 64 (1993), 348–371.

40 Alan M. Leslie, 'Children's understanding of the mental world,' in *The Oxford Companion to the Mind*, ed. Richard L. Gregory (Oxford: Oxford University Press, 1987), 139–142.

41 Baron-Cohen, 'Theory of mind in normal development and autism.'

42 Lillard, 'Pretend play skills and the child's theory of mind,' 348.

43 Kornei Chukovsky, *From Two to Five*, trans. and ed. Miriam Morton (Berkeley, CA: University of California Press, 1963), 98–101.

3 Language play and nonsense

Diddle, diddle, dumpling, my son John,
Went to bed with his trousers on;
One shoe off, and the other shoe on,
Diddle, diddle, dumpling, my son John.

3.1 Playing with language

Language play manipulates the rules of linguistic discourse. Phonology, morphology, syntax and semantics, sociolinguistic rules, codes and context are all fair game.[1] Linguistic play is a self-absorbed activity, preoccupied with revealing, and interrogating, its constituent parts. In its most extravagant form – the genre of literary nonsense – it creates such an abundance of meaning that it signifies nothing at all. I will have more to say about nonsense later.

Language play is a metalinguistic game that everyone plays.[2] It is at the center of parent–child communication[3] and it is crucial for language learning. Babies delight in wordgames, especially when the wonderful rhythms are accompanied by another's touch. Nursery rhymes and nonsense verses, finger games, lullabies and jingles are the playful repertoire of the very young.

These are games that are played over and over. The importance of rhythmic intonation and repetition in this process cannot be overemphasized: we know that 'familiarity through repetition inscribes the territory until it is known by heart.'[4] The baby, for his part, responds with long sequences of vocal modulation, humming, chanting and tuneless songs.[5]

Purely phonological play begins to diversify and sounds acquire symbolic value as the child begins to construct the protolinguistic models she needs to realize different intentions. Rhythm and rhyme, the most prominent characteristics of nursery rhymes and caregiver baby talk, tend to be the first features of language which are consciously manipulated by children.

> Children who have just begun to talk in phrases make use of rhyme to ease the task of pronouncing two words in a row. It is easier for the very young child to say 'night-night' than 'good night.' It seems the younger the child the greater the attraction to word repetition that rhymes.[6]

A little later, children begin to pay attention to some of the other linguistic features of nursery rhymes. The structure of the nursery rhyme makes it easy to remember; its regular rhyme scheme and metrical pattern is simple and straightforward.

Jack be nimble,
Jack be quick,
Jack jump over
The candlestick.

Rub-a-dub-dub
Three men in a tub,
And who do you think they be?
The butcher, the baker,
The candlestick-maker,
Turn 'em out, knaves all three.

By foregrounding form and structure in this way, nursery rhymes enable young children to learn a great deal about the structure of language. This knowledge serves as a strong foundation for further discoveries. As they become attuned to the formal patterns and grammatical parallelism typical of nursery rhymes, children begin to pay attention to semantic and pragmatic features, supplying their own meanings when they encounter words they do not understand.[7]

It is only when the meaning of the rhyme begins to become transparent that children begin to lose interest in nursery rhymes and seek other world-creating forms of language play. This raises a number of interesting issues.

First, there appears to be a direct correlation between the patterning of form and the creation of imaginary characters and hypothetical worlds. The foregrounding of formal patterns allows 'possibilities to emerge which might otherwise have been eliminated by force of the habitual.'[8] The pattern establishes the ground rules of the game and serves to convey the basic ludic message 'this is [language] play.'

The second point, mentioned in Chapter 2, is that children's enjoyment of pretence is dependent on the extent to which they are aware of the self-deception and are capable of recognizing play as play. Once they have exhausted the relatively limited possibilities offered by the nursery rhyme genre, children move on to more challenging and subversive forms of wordplay which bend the phonological, syntactic or semantic rules of speech through the use of repetition and reversals, embedding, substitution and other playful techniques. Since the aim is to be as subversive as possible, parody and impropriety rule.

Traditional nursery rhymes generally give way to longer sequences which play with the notion of repetition in various ways. Many of these wordgames employ complex patterns of accumulation and embedding to build narrative suspense:

> In a dark, dark wood, there was a dark, dark house,
> And in that dark, dark house there was a dark, dark room,
> And in that dark, dark room, there was a dark, dark cupboard,
> And in that dark, dark cupboard, there was a dark, dark shelf,
> And on that dark, dark shelf, there was a dark, dark box,
> And in that dark, dark box, there was a GHOST!

Chain verses of this kind are a perennial feature of children's wordplay. The cumulative tale of 'The House That Jack Built' is probably the best known example of this particular playform. The fact that the story has so very little to say about the house, or about Jack, and is so rich in every other detail adds immeasurably to the pleasure of the text. Here is an early version:

> This is the house that Jack built.
>
> This is the malt that lay in the house that Jack built.
>
> This is the rat, that ate the malt that lay in the house that Jack built.
>
> This is the cat, that killed the rat, that ate the malt that lay in the house that Jack built.
>
> ...
>
> This is the farmer sowing his corn, that kept the cock that crowed in the morn, that waked the priest all shaven and shorn, that married the man all tattered and torn, that kissed the maiden all forlorn, that milked the cow with the crumpled horn, that tossed the dog, that

worried the cat, that killed the rat, that ate the malt that lay in the house that Jack built.

Chain verses, with their deeply embedded relative clauses, are endlessly fascinating in the way they play with beginnings and endings, cause and effect. For the moment I wish to focus on the dialogical dimension of these elaborate games and the techniques players use in different kinds of verbal play.

While nursery rhymes build on the interactive patterns of rhythm and rhyme which characterize infant–caregiver baby talk, chain verses and similar language games strengthen and diversify the interpersonal dimensions of language play in a number of ways. Tested and refined in the playground,[9] these verses demand an audience for maximum impact. As rhymes are passed on from one child to another and from one generation to the next, they build new relationships between players each time they are performed.

These playforms also allow for the bending and breaking of conventional linguistic rules, a process which, as we have already observed, performs an essentially metalinguistic function. As Crystal and other linguists have pointed out, the greater a child's ability to play with language, the more advanced his or her command of language will be.[10]

By the age of six, children tend to have quite a wide-ranging repertoire of language games. Tongue twisters and knock-knock games become popular, and storytelling proves to be a reliable way of making friends.

> The kingpins of the playground are the tellers of jokes and stories … Their material is very various. 'Jokes' covers almost any form of verbal fun. To children a 'joke' is seldom the kind of miniature comic story told by comedians, most often it is a question with a clever answer that must be guessed, which, if pressed, they would say was a 'riddle.'[11]

The riddle may, of course, take many forms. It may be a poetic rhyming riddle –

> Riddle me, riddle me, what is that,
> Over the head, and under the hat? (Hair)

> It is a little house,
> It has a hundred windows
> Yet it won't hold a mouse (A spider's web)

– or a pun masquerading as a riddle:

> What has teeth but cannot bite? A comb.

> What key is hardest to turn? A don-key.

The most common form, however, is the conundrum. Conundrums also depend on puns for their comic effect. They usually pose the question 'What is the difference between *x* and *y*?'

> What is the difference between a big, black cloud and a lion with a toothache?
> One pours with rain and the other roars with pain.

> Why did the lobster blush? – Because it saw the salad dressing.

'Trick' riddles ('Why did the chicken cross the road?') always have a banal, common-sense answer. Wellerisms,[12] on the other hand, ridicule the common-sense meanings of proverbs or well-known expressions. ('What did the big chimney say to the little chimney?' 'You're too young to smoke.')

Riddles (even silly ones such as these) merge separate worlds of meaning by setting up one frame of reference and then replacing it with another. Riddles are interrogative, dialogical playforms which actually transform one world into another.[13] This explains why they are often associated with ritual practices that seek to reverse the everyday order of things and to turn one thing into something else.[14]

Conundrums, as in the cloud and lion example cited above, extend the notion of reversal by offering a solution made up of two symmetrical parts, each one 'a linguistic inversion of the other'.[15] There may be real world differences between clouds and lions, but the only differences that count in this instance are linguistic ones. Wellerisms, however, subvert expectations by enabling a metaphorical phrase to be interpreted literally. This has the unsettling effect of undercutting both types of meaning at the same time.

As mentioned, riddles often feature puns. Puns manipulate the disorientation that is created when two or more worlds of meaning coexist within one word. Puns work by offering 'alternative patterns, one apparent and one hidden,'[16] and by bringing the latter to the surface in a way that challenges common sense meaning.[17] Unlike metaphors, with which they are closely associated, puns need not be especially creative playforms. They have a limited number of meanings (usually only two), and they do their best work in tightly controlled environments such as nonsense texts.

We also encounter the merging of worlds in graphic wordgames such as rebuses, acrostics, calligrams and ambigrams. Rebuses achieve their effect by mixing words and images in startling ways. The term *rebus* (from the Latin, meaning 'by things') refers to the representation of a word or syllable by a figure, symbol or picture of an object with a similar name. Pictures and symbols are chosen purely on the basis of sound, not semantics, and the challenge is to decipher the puzzle's true meaning.

Acrostics and calligrams are linguistic playforms which overflow with meaning. Both of them are 'forms that take on an added dimension through the process of reading the text on the page.'[18] In the word pictures known as *calligrams* ('calligram' is a contraction of 'calligraphy' and 'ideogram'), form recreates meaning – with the result that meaning is doubly inscribed. The mouse's 'long and sad tail/tale' in *Alice's Adventures in Wonderland* is the most celebrated calligram in children's literature.

Acrostics also play with double meanings. The *acrostic* (from the Greek: *akros*, 'at the end' and *stikhos*, 'of the row') is a poem in which the initial letters of each line can be read sequentially to form a message of some kind. Acrostics are particularly interesting in the way they foreground the process of reading.

This early-nineteenth-century acrostic alphabet doubles as a nursery rhyme:

An Apple Pie

A   was an Apple Pie
B   Bit it
C   Cut it
D   Dealt it
E   Eat it
F   Fought for it
G   Got it
H   Had it
I   Inspected it
J   Jumped for it
K   Kept it
L   Longed for it
M   Mourned for it
N   Nodded at it
O   Opened it

P Peeped in it
Q Quartered it
R Ran for it
S Stole it
T Took it
U Upset it
V Viewed it
W Wanted it
X, Y, Z and ampersand
all wished for a piece in hand.

We now come to the most extreme form of graphic language play: the *ambigram* (literally, an 'all around image' or FlipScript™). Ambigrams are 'designed to be read upside down, back to front or in a mirror – as well as their usual way (in English, from left to right.)'[19] While certain words, such as 'suns' or 'dollop', form natural ambigrams, others reveal ambigrammatic possibilities with clever typographic manipulation, as in the spectacular ambigram created by John Langdon for the title of his book, *Wordplay*.[20]

Collapsing the boundaries between word and image, the ambigram takes us to the outer limits of language play. But this is not the end of the matter. I will conclude this discussion of wordplay with the most innovative of all linguistic playforms: literary nonsense. In the following section I focus on the defining characteristics of nonsense and look at the techniques employed by the masters of nonsense literature, Lewis Carroll and Edward Lear.

3.2 Nonsense

Nonsense (literally meaning 'words that make no sense') is the most radical form of linguistic play. Nonsense actually makes too much sense. It is outrageously, excessively meaningful. 'In nonsense, metaphor runs rampant until there is wall-to-wall metaphor and thus wall-to-wall literalness.'[21] Lifting words out of context to create an untranslatable system which compromises the status of words as linguistic signs,[22] nonsense conveys a multiplicity of meaning within a strictly circumscribed playframe, a self-contained world which deflects all attempts to impose interpretative order from the outside.

If we take the great nonsense poem 'Jabberwocky' as our point of entry into the world of literary nonsense, it may be instructive to approach the text in exactly the same way Alice does. When she steps through the looking-glass she finds that all real world systems of classification, hierarchy, direction and scale have been reversed.

Figure 5 From *Through the Looking-Glass*, illustration by John Tenniel

Alice has to hold the text up to the mirror to read what's written on the page. The words reflected back to her have a strangely hypnotic quality. Here is the famous first (and last) stanza:

'Twas brillig, and the slithy toves
Did gyre and gimble in the wabe;
All mimsy were the borogoves,
And the mome raths outgrabe.[23]

As a poem, 'Jabberwocky' is thoroughly conventional in almost every respect. It is quite straightforward phonetically and its syntax is coherent. Words are formed in a regular way and the grammatical structure is clear. Rhythm, rhyme and meter create a haunting if slightly discordant melody which 'chimes with subtle overtones.'[24] The only problem, as Alice points out, is that none of it makes sense.

'It seems rather pretty,' she said when she had finished it, 'but it's rather hard to understand!' (You see she didn't like to confess, even to herself, that she couldn't make it out at all.) 'Somehow it seems to fill my head with ideas – only I don't exactly know what they are!'[25]

'Jabberwocky' defies the rules of semantics to produce a text which overflows with meaning. In this, it is a microcosm of the topsy-turvy looking-glass world where the rules of time and space have been suspended and the normal order of things no longer applies.

'Jabberwocky' demonstrates many of the characteristic maneuvers of nonsense literature. To appreciate the extent of its achievement, we need to pause for a moment and consider the methods employed by nonsense to interrogate common sense meaning. The following list is not exhaustive but it does demonstrate the range of operations which come into play in literary nonsense:

- play with reversals and inversions;
- play with the boundaries of discourse;
- play with simultaneity;
- arrangement and rearrangement within a closed field; and
- play with embedding and infinite repetition.[26]

Play with reversals and inversions

Nonsense is obsessed with the organization of knowledge and it often inverts and transposes categories (living and non-living; animal and human) to startling effect. In Edward Lear's nonsense stories we encounter singularities such as the old man of Blackheath ('whose head was adorned with a wreath, of lobsters and spice, pickled onions and mice, that uncommon old man of Blackheath'); the Co-operative Cauliflower (who 'being able to walk tolerably well with a fluctuating and graceful movement on a single cabbage stalk' was saved 'the expense of stockings and shoes'); and the unfortunate heroes of *The Adventures of Mr Lear, the Polly and the Pusseybite on their way to the Ritertitle Mountains,* who tumble over a waterfall and are dashed to bits. The trio is reassembled, but imperfectly, and not, as Lear puts it matter-of-factly, 'as three individuals.'[27]

Equally disorienting is the tendency in nonsense texts to disregard distinctions between living creatures and inanimate/mechanical objects. Consider Alice's predicament in *Alice's Adventures in Wonderland* when she attempts to play croquet with agitated hoops, balls and mallets:

I don't think they play at all fairly ... and they don't seem to have any rules in particular; at least if there are, nobody attends to them – and you've no idea how confusing it is all the things being alive: for instance, there's the arch I've got to go through next walking about at the other end of the ground – and I should have croqueted the Queen's hedgehog just now, only it ran away when it saw mine coming![28]

This is only part of the story, of course. In Wonderland, all of the members of the royal family, together with their attendants and courtiers, soldiers and gardeners, are *objects* – playing cards – transformed into sentient beings, inhabitants of a fictional playworld which is, in itself, an intertextual recreation of another kingdom: the nursery rhyme world of 'The Queen of Hearts.'

While nonsense texts are strictly conservative in form and structure, they have no time for moralizing or affectation. Nonsense exults in parody. The *Alice* poems, in particular, delight in turning didactic poetry into sheer nonsense. Robert Southey's 'The old man's comforts and how he gained them' –

'You are old, father William,' the young man cried,
'The few locks which are left you are grey;
You are hale, father William, a hearty old man;
Now tell me the reason, I pray.'
'In the days of my youth,' father William replied,
'I remember'd that youth would fly fast,
And abus'd not my health and my vigour at first,
That I never might need them at last'...

– is turned upside down when Alice recites it:

'You are old, Father William,' the young man said,
'And your hair has become very white;
And yet you incessantly stand on your head –
Do you think, at your age, it is right?'
'In my youth,' Father William replied to his son,
'I feared it might injure the brain;
But now that I'm perfectly sure I have none,
Why, I do it again and again'...

Other memorable examples include:

'Speak gently' **(G. W. Langford)**	**'Speak roughly to your little boy'** **(Lewis Carroll)**
Speak gently! It is better far To rule by love than fear; Speak gently; let no harsh words mar The good we might do here! ...	Speak roughly to your little boy And beat him till he sneezes, He only does it to annoy, Because he knows it teases ...

'Against idleness and mischief' **(Isaac Watts)**	**'How doth the little crocodile'** **(Lewis Carroll)**
How doth the little busy bee Improve each shining hour And gather honey all the day From every opening flower! How skilfully she builds her cell! How neat she spreads her wax! And labours hard to store it well With the sweet food she makes.	How doth the little crocodile Improve his shining tail, And pour the waters of the Nile On every golden scale! How cheerfully he seems to grin, And neatly spreads his claws, And welcomes little fishes in, With gently smiling jaws!

Nonsensical play with reversals and inversions can be seen in reversible texts such as *palindromes* (words or phrases which read the same backwards and forwards; 'palindrome' is from the Greek, *palindromos*, meaning 'running back'), conundrums, and self-denying discourse that consumes itself as it proceeds, as in the Mock Turtle's schedule:

'And how many hours a day did you do lessons?' said Alice, in a hurry to change the subject.

'Ten hours the first day,' said the Mock Turtle: 'Nine the next, and so on.'

'What a curious plan!' exclaimed Alice.

'That's the reason they're called lessons,' the gryphon remarked: 'because they lessen from day to day.'...

'Then the eleventh day must have been a holiday?'

'Of course it was,' said the Mock Turtle.

'And how did you manage on the twelfth?' Alice went on eagerly.

'That's enough about lessons,' the Gryphon interrupted in a very decided tone. 'Tell her something about the games now.'[29]

Play with boundaries

Play with the boundaries of discourse challenges the limits of things, producing a surplus of meaningful information. As mentioned in my discussion of language play, playforms such as ambigrams, acrostics and calligrams all work in this way, acquiring added dimensions of meaning as we read on. These boundary-breaking devices are frequently found in nonsense literature.

Edward Lear's nonsense botanies and zoologies play with the boundaries of scientific classification. These joyful creations take the form of ingenious visual puns.

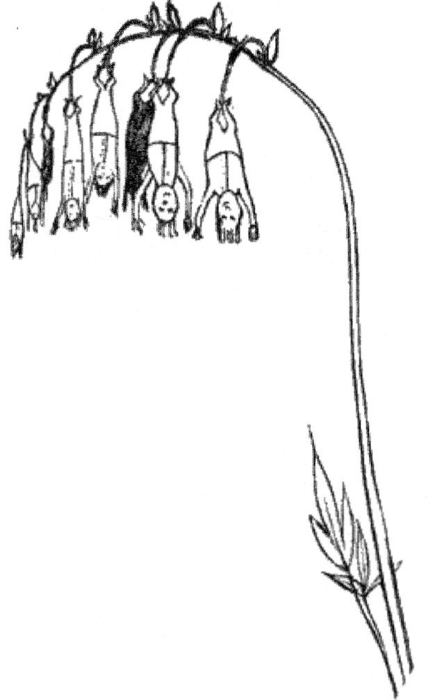

Figure 6 'Manypeeplia upsidownia' from *Nonsense Botany* by Edward Lear

Figure 7 'Piggiwiggia pyramidalis' from *Nonsense Botany* by Edward Lear

Play with simultaneity

As noted previously, riddles, jokes and puns involve the simultaneity of two or more meanings within a single word or proposition. The conflation/ superimposition of worlds which results from this process is characteristic of all forms of pretend play.

Martin Gardner, the editor of *The Annotated Alice*, remarks that the *Alice* stories 'swarm with puns.'[30] Here are just a few. Emerging from the pool of tears, Alice and her companions need to 'dry' themselves as quickly as possible. The Mouse proceeds to recite a passage from *A Short Course of History*, 'the driest thing I know.' The Mouse's 'long and sad tale' resembles a 'tail.' The tail may or may 'not' be tied in a 'knot.' Alice learns that 'Mock Turtle Soup' is made from a 'Mock Turtle,' and that the Mock Turtle and the Gryphon called their school master 'Tortoise' because he 'taught us.' Their 'lessons' were described as such because they became shorter and shorter every day.

Puns can be equally amusing when they fall flat. Here is the King considering the White Rabbit's evidence:

'Nothing can be clearer than *that.* Then again – "*before she had this fit –*" you never had fits, my dear, I think?' he said to the Queen.

'Never!' said the Queen, furiously, throwing an inkstand at the Lizard as she spoke …

'Then the words don't *fit* you,' said the King, looking around the court with a smile. There was a dead silence.

'It's a pun!' the King added in angry tone, and everybody laughed.[31]

The Alice stories are also packed with portmanteau words, so named because Humpty Dumpty defined them that way.

'Well, "*slithy*" means "lithe and slimy." "Lithe" is the same as "active." You see it's like a portmanteau[32] – there are two meanings packed up into one word.'

'I see it now,' Alice remarked thoughtfully: 'and what are "*toves*"?'

'Well, "*toves*" are something like badgers – they're something like lizards and they're something like corkscrews.'[33]

Carroll offers numerous riddles for Alice to solve. The longest, expressed in the form of a 'true' rhyming riddle, is posed by the White Queen:

> 'First, the fish must be caught.'
> That is easy: a baby, I think, would have caught it.
> 'Next, the fish must be bought.'
> That is easy: a penny, I think, would have bought it.
>
> 'Now cook me the fish!'
> That is easy, and will not take more than a minute.
> 'Let it lie in a dish!'
> That is easy, because it already is in it.
>
> 'Bring it here! Let me sup!'
> It is easy to set such a dish on the table.
> 'Take the dish-cover up!'
> Ah, *that* is so hard that I fear I'm unable!
>
> For it holds it like glue –
> Holds the lid to the dish, while it lies in the middle:
> Which is easiest to do,
> Un-dish-cover the fish, or dishcover the riddle?[34]

The most infuriating is posed by the Mad Hatter:

> 'Why is a raven like a writing desk?'
> …
> 'I give it up,' Alice replied. 'What's the answer?'
> 'I haven't the slightest idea,' said the Hatter.
> 'Nor I,' said the March Hare.[35]

Arrangement and rearrangement within a closed field

The practitioners of nonsense often appropriate predetermined systems and structures for their own ends. We have seen how some nonsense procedures play with the boundaries of discourse; here we have the opposite approach: preserving the boundaries of discourse while scorning its other elements. Anagrams are obvious examples, as are secret languages and rebuses, where components can be combined and recombined in countless ways. Literary parodies, mentioned briefly above, may also be considered from this point of view.

The discourse of make-believe play and games is perfectly suited to this kind of arrangement. Carroll exploits the many possibilities of parlor games and puzzles, games of chess and playing cards, contests, races and other outdoor games. Characters may be poor at taking turns, and they often move around in unorthodox ways, but they do observe the basic rules of the game, as the author's explanation of the chess moves in *The Looking-Glass* demonstrates.[36] Carroll also ensures that his playing-card characters are portrayed with the utmost verisimilitude. As Martin Gardner has noted:

> Among the spot cards the spades are the gardeners, the clubs are soldiers, diamonds are courtiers, and the hearts are the ten royal children. The court cards are of course members of the court. Note how cleverly Carroll has linked the behaviour of his animated cards with the behaviour of actual playing cards. They lie flat on their faces, they cannot be identified from their backs, they are easily turned over, and they bend themselves into croquet arches.[37]

Nonsense writers are also drawn to self-contained classification systems (the dictionary and the encyclopedia) and institutions (zoological gardens and herbaria, museums and archives) which organize knowledge in ways that can seem quite unfathomable to outsiders. Carroll and Lear shared the Victorians' fascination with taxonomy, list making and categorization, and these influences can be seen throughout their work.

> 'You may call it "nonsense" if you like … but *I've* heard nonsense, compared with which that would be as sensible as a dictionary' said the Red Queen.[38]

****

> 'Half-way up that bush you'll see a Rocking-horse-fly, if you look. It's made entirely of wood, and it gets about by swinging itself from branch to branch.'
>
> 'What does it live on?' Alice asked, with great curiosity.
>
> 'Sap and sawdust,' said the Gnat. 'Go on with the list.'
>
> Alice looked at the Rocking-horse fly with great interest, and made up her mind that it must have been just repainted, it looked so bright and sticky …[39]

Figure 8 From *Through the Looking-Glass*, illustration by John Tenniel

Play with infinity

Play with infinity, or with infinite repetition and embedding, involves a specific form of boundary manipulation: the manipulation of expectations about beginnings and endings. Devices such as repetition, circularity, nesting and embedding, the series and the causal chain may all be enlisted to interrogate notions of closure and causality.

'Jabberwocky', the poem with which I began this brief discussion of nonsense literature, illustrates this procedure. 'Jabberwocky' is a traditional quest[40] without a resolution. Its circular structure condemns it to endless repetition in true nonsense form.

On the other hand, a nonsense series such as this one:

> 'They were learning to draw,' the Dormouse went on … 'and they
> drew all manner of things – everything that begins with an M – '
> 'Why with an M?' said Alice.
> 'Why not?' said the March Hare …
> The Dormouse … went on: ' – that begins with an M, such as
> mouse-traps, and the moon, and memory, and muchness – you
> know you say things are "much of a muchness" – did you ever see
> such a thing as a drawing of a muchness!'[41]

has no logical starting point and could go on forever.

The Red King's dream, as interpreted by Tweedledee, plays with the notion of infinity in a number of ways.

Figure 9 From *Through The Looking-Glass*, illustration by John Tenniel

'He [the Red King] [is] dreaming now,' said Tweedledee: 'and what do you think he's dreaming about?'

Alice said 'Nobody can guess that.'

'Why, about you!' Tweedledee exclaimed, clapping his hands triumphantly. 'And if he left off dreaming about you, where do you suppose you'd be?'

'Where I am now, of course,' said Alice.

'Not you!' Tweedledee retorted contemptuously. 'You'd be nowhere. Why you're only a sort of a thing in his dream!'[42]

The Red King's dream is actually a dream within a dream: Alice is dreaming of the Red King, who is dreaming of Alice, and so on. The dream motif functions as a *mise en abyme*, a figurative device often used in nonsense texts and metafictions to highlight a thematic or structural element of the narrative by representing it in miniature. The fictional world, and everything in it, *is* a dream, of course, just as it had been in Wonderland.

There is a paradox at work here which highlights the playful nature of Carroll's work. The Red King's dream is an embedded text, a story within another story, which simultaneously represents the possibility of infinity by inverting the common-sense procedure of definition by closure *and* challenges the notion of infinity by presenting closure *repeated*.[43]

Its reflexive tendencies carry nonsense into the literary domains of playful metafiction and intertextuality. In the following chapters, I focus on the experience of reading playful texts and look at some outstanding texts for young readers. Some of these narratives employ nonsense strategies; all of them play with words and/or images in inventive and imaginative ways.

Notes

1 Barbara Kirshenblatt-Gimblett and Joel Sherzer, 'Introduction to speech play,' in *Speech Play*, 7–8. Also see Linda A. Holmes, 'Language play as response discourse,' *Language Arts* 76(3) (1999), 259.

2 For a detailed study of the metalinguistic features of language play, see Courtney B. Cazden, 'Play with language and meta-linguistic awareness: one dimension of language experience,' in *Play – Its Role in Development and Evolution*, eds. Jerome S. Bruner, Alison Jolly and Kathy Sylva (Harmondsworth: Penguin Books, 1976), 603–608.

3 See Kornei Chukovsky, *From Two to Five*, trans. and ed. Miriam Morton (Berkeley, CA: University of California Press, 1963); David Crystal, *Language Play* (Harmondsworth: Penguin Books, 1998), 159.

4 Marina Warner, *No Go the Bogeyman: Scaring, Lulling and Making Mock* (London: Chatto and Windus, 1998), 204.

5 Crystal, *Language Play*, 164.

6 Chukovsky, *From Two to Five*, 63.

7 Guy Cook, *Language Play, Language Learning* (Oxford: Oxford University Press, 2000), 25.

8 Ibid., 48. Susan Stewart reaches a similar conclusion in her extensive study of nonsense forms: *Nonsense: Aspects of Intertextuality in Folklore and Literature* (Baltimore, MD: Johns Hopkins University Press, 1978).

9 As demonstrated by the landmark studies conducted by Iona and Peter Opie, *The Lore and Language of Schoolchildren* (Oxford: Oxford University Press, 1959) and by Iona Opie, *The People in the Playground* (Oxford: Oxford University Press, 1993).

10 Crystal, *Language Play*, 181.

11 Iona Opie, *The People in the Playground*, 13. This book is my main source for the various types of riddles heard in the playground.

12 Named after Sam Weller and his father, characters in *The Pickwick Papers*.

13 This perspective is examined in detail by Galit Hasan-Rokem and David Shulman in their introduction to *Untying the Knot: On Riddles and Other Enigmatic Modes*, op. cit., 3–9.

14 See, particularly, Don Handelman, 'Traps of trans-formation: theoretical convergences between riddle and ritual', in *Untying the Knot*, 37–61.

15 Stewart, *Nonsense*, 69.

16 Mary Douglas, 'Jokes', in *Implicit Meanings: Essays in Anthropology* (London: Routledge and Kegan Paul, 1975), 95.

17 Ibid., 95; Cook, *Language Play, Language Learning*, 84.

18 Stewart, *Nonsense*, 97.

19 Crystal, *Language Play*, 154.

20 John Langdon, *Wordplay: The Philosophy, Art, and Science of Ambigrams* (New York: Harcourt Brace Jovanovich, 1992).

21 Stewart, *Nonsense*, 35.

22 Kirshenblatt-Gimblett, 'Speech play and verbal art', in *Play and Learning*, ed. Brian Sutton-Smith (New York: Gardner Press, 1979), 223–224.

23 Lewis Carroll, *Through the Looking-Glass and What Alice Found There*, Chapter 1. This and all subsequent extracts from *Through the Looking-Glass* are from the Project Gutenberg eBook of *Through the Looking-Glass* available at www.gutenberg.org/files/12/12-h/12-h.htm

24 Martin Gardner, in the notes to 'Jabberwocky' in his edition of Lewis Carroll, *Through the Looking-Glass*, in *The Annotated Alice: The Definitive Edition*, *Alice's Adventures in Wonderland* and *Through the Looking-Glass*, illustrated by John Tenniel, ed. Martin Gardner (Harmondsworth: Penguin Books, 2001), 192, note 11, and in *The Annotated Alice: The Definitive Edition, Alice's Adventures in Wonderland* and *Through the Looking-Glass*, illustrated by John Tenniel, ed. Martin Gardner (New York: W. W. Norton, 2000), 149, note 11.

 For detail on the prosody of 'Jabberwocky' see Marnie Parsons, *Touch Monkeys: Nonsense Strategies for Reading Twentieth Century Poetry* (University of Toronto Press, 1994) 67–73. Parsons observes that the use of regular iambic tetrameter in the first three lines of each stanza is consistently undercut by trimeter in the fourth. This has an unsettling effect on a reader already struggling to find meaning in the poem.

25 *Through the Looking-Glass*, chapter 1. For more on Alice's confession, see Jean-Jacques Lecercle, *Philosophy of Nonsense: The intuitions of Victorian nonsense literature* (London: Routledge, 1994), 22: 'This is the best description I know of the experience of reading nonsense. What Alice is dimly aware of is that narrative coherence somehow compensates [in nonsense] for semantic incoherence.'

26 Based on Stewart, *Nonsense*, 51, 57–193; and Wim Tigges, 'An anatomy of nonsense', in *Explorations in the Field of Nonsense*, ed. Wim Tigges (Amsterdam: Rodopi, 1987), 27.

27 Edward Lear, *The Adventures of Mr Lear, the Polly and the Pusseybite on their way to the Ritertitle Mountains.* Private correspondence, dated August 23, 1866

and published posthumously. Available at www.nonsenselit.org/Lear/pw/riter.
html

28 Lewis Carroll, *Alice's Adventures in Wonderland*, Chapter 8. This and all subsequent extracts from *Alice's Adventures in Wonderland* are from the Project Gutenberg eBook at www.gutenberg.org/files/11/11-h/11-h.htm

29 *Alice's Adventures in Wonderland*, chapter 9.

30 See Gardner's note, *The Annotated Alice*, Penguin edition, 129; W. W. Norton edition, 98.

31 *Alice's Adventures in Wonderland*, chapter 12.

32 Portmanteau, or port, is a synonym for suitcase.

33 *Through the Looking-Glass*, chapter 6. Humpty Dumpty is helping Alice make sense of 'Jabberwocky'.

34 Ibid., chapter 9. The answer: an oyster.

35 *Alice in Wonderland*, chapter 7.

36 See the Preface to *Through the Looking-Glass*, *The Annotated Alice*, Penguin, 171–172; Norton, 133–134.

37 Gardner, *The Annotated Alice*, Penguin, 107, note 1; Norton, 81, note 2.

38 *Through the Looking-Glass*, chapter 2.

39 Ibid., chapter 3.

40 In this it also anticipates that much darker existential quest, *The Hunting of the Snark*, which references the earlier text in numerous ways. In the Preface to *The Hunting of the Snark*, Lewis Carroll takes pains to explain the correct pronunciation of the 'hard' words in 'Jabberwocky' and to support Humpty Dumpty's portmanteau semantics. The *Snark* contains many of Jabberwocky's portmanteaux, including: 'beamish', 'uffish', 'galumphing', 'outgrabe', 'the Bandersnatch', 'fruminous', and 'mimsy'.

41 *Alice's Adventures in Wonderland*, Chapter 7.

42 *Through the Looking-Glass*, Chapter 4.

43 See Stewart, *Nonsense*, 125–129, 202.

4   Interacting with texts

And that's when it dawned on Herb that he had fallen into the book … 'Whoops! I'm so sorry,' squeaked Herb terrified. 'I didn't mean to be here.' 'Oh, that's quite all right,' said the largest bear. 'It could happen to anyone.' 'And does all the time,' said the small bear, scowling at Goldilocks.

Lauren Child, Who's Afraid of the Big Bad Book?[1]

4.1 Collaborations

To learn to read a book, as distinct from simply recognizing words or images on a page, young readers must become

> both *the teller* (picking up the author's voice and point of view) and *the told* (the recipient of the story and its interpreter). This symbolic interaction is learned early. It is rarely, if ever, taught, except in so far as an adult stands in for the author by giving the text a 'voice' when reading to the child.[2]

During early book-reading and storytelling sessions, the adult engages and sustains the child's involvement by continually encouraging him to build on what has been learned in previous sessions, and inviting him to infer new meanings from the text they are reading together. Jerome Bruner has conceptualized the making of meaning in these contexts as a collaborative transaction in which the adult serves as a kind of vicarious consciousness, enabling the child to make far greater leaps than would have been possible otherwise.[3] Scaffolding techniques, as Bruner describes them, include questions, comments, exclamations and repeated confirmation of the child's reactions.

The experience of being told a story, and of 'reading', can, for the first nine months or so, hardly be differentiated from conversation, play, and other interactions with parents, older brothers and sisters, and other caregivers ... For the child at this age, just learning to distinguish the outside world from inner experience, story listening would seem to be another route by which trusted adults initiate him or her into what is rapidly becoming the other world outside.[4]

Infants respond to reading and storytelling as they do to other playful forms of communication, moving to the rhythm of the reader's voice, making eye contact, and following her gestures as she points to images on the page. As their acts of meaning become more diverse and they become more practiced in the world-creating functions of imaginative play, children pretend to read from favorite books and act out stories that have been read to them, sometimes enlisting toys as fellow actors. The action in these make-believe scripts usually goes well beyond the original story line, transforming the narrative in unexpected ways.[5]

Interaction with stories and other readers teaches important reading lessons. Rather than simply focusing on the names of objects, young readers begin to make textual connections, asking questions about what is happening in the text as a whole, and making observations about absent objects, past events and other decontextualized features.[6] Drawing on insights gleaned from make-believe play, young children can discern the 'let's pretend' element of narrative fiction and respond accordingly. They become increasingly aware of the boundary between the fictional and pragmatic worlds and, with the assistance of older readers, ever more confident in negotiating the world of the story.

Margaret Meek characterizes the reading process as 'an elaborate game with rules.'[7] In *How Texts Teach What Readers Learn*, she focuses on picturebooks by authors such as Pat Hutchins, John Burningham, Anthony Browne and the Ahlbergs, all of whom leave gaps or puzzles to be solved/discovered by the reader in dialogue with the text.

Pat Hutchins's fable, *Rosie's Walk*,[8] is a fine example. The story is straightforward. Rosie, the little red hen, leaves her hen house and goes for a walk. Apparently unaware of the fox who is stalking her every step, Rosie leads her pursuer through a punishing obstacle course where each trial is nastier than the last. In an important case study, Margaret Meek and her young co-reader, Ben, work together to reveal the reading secrets of *Rosie's Walk*. Those secrets are hidden in the words *and* the pictures, and readers have to pay close attention to both. Does Rosie know that the fox is after her? Maybe not, but she does take the long, long way home (*across* the yard, then *around, over, past, through, under* and *back* again). What is more, the interrelationship of word and image is one of delicate counterpoint, producing a simple but richly ironic text.

As Margaret Meek concludes, 'The essential lesson of *Rosie's Walk* depends on there being no mention of the fox, but the reader knows there would be no story without him. Nowhere but in a reader's interaction with a text can this lesson be learned.'[9]

So, how should we characterize this interaction? The literary theorist Wolfgang Iser contends that meaning and significance reside in the encounter *between* reader and text – an encounter which he describes as essentially playful.[10]

For Iser, a literary text is a system of response-inviting structures, 'meaning-assembly instructions,' which the reader must activate in order to make sense of the narrative.[11] The literary text must be conceived in such a way that it engages the reader's imagination in the creative task of working things out for her or himself.[12]

It follows that '[t]he text can never be grasped as a whole – only as a series of changing viewpoints, each one restricted in itself and so necessitating further perspectives. This is the process by which the reader "realizes" an overall situation.'[13] In fact, it is the need to accommodate multiple, changing perspectives, to make connections and to account, in some way, for the numerous gaps and indeterminacies left in the text that entices the reader to participate both in the production and the comprehension – the 'performance' – of meaning.[14] Barthes says something similar when he insists that the reader plays the text 'twice,' playing, interactively, as one plays a game and playing as one plays a musical score, in a 'practical collaboration.'[15]

Iser also emphasizes the transformative aspects of engaging with literary texts, drawing another parallel between reading and play. As mentioned earlier, the reader must continually make choices from the range of possibilities offered by the text. As a result, both reader and text undergo profound changes during a reading performance.

Active readers, like players, must commit to the interactive process in which they are participating.[16] This has powerful implications for children's reading since young readers who are alert to their role as readers and aware of themselves as conscious agents in a transactional process are also more likely to be aware of the many influences at work in a narrative.

4.2 Reading dialogically

We can now say with confidence that literary reading is an interactive process – a dialogue, if you like – which transforms the reader and the text. Learning to read dialogically, in the way that Meek, following Mikhail Bakhtin, uses the term,[17] attunes the reader to intricate textual patterns that might otherwise elude detection. Dialogical reading seeks out potential connections between disparate materials[18] – allowing readers to interrogate the relations of similarity, contiguity and interconnectivity that exist between things in time and space.[19] Before looking at this process in action, I wish to sketch some of the key features of Mikhail Bakhtin's dialogical perspective.

For Bakhtin, a text or utterance comprises multiple points of view (Bakhtin refers to a 'polyphony' of voices), each existing in some kind of relation to the others. It is interesting to note that young children can be quite sensitive to this dimension of textual meaning, perceiving words as 'voices' on the page.[20]

As far as the reader is concerned, this 'multi-voicedness' consists of the play of narrative voices and viewpoints within the text and the play of inter-texts (implicitly or explicitly quoted/borrowed words, images or concepts) with which the text engages and within which it is situated.[21] (As we will see in the next chapter, intertextuality is a defining feature of playful texts. *Rosie's Walk*, for example, is an intertextual mosaic which reflects, directly or indirectly, influences as diverse as *The Canterbury Tales*, Aesop's Fables, 'Chicken-Licken' and 'The Little Red Hen', silent movies of the 20s and 30s, folk art and decorative painting.)

The dialogue between reader and text is also shaped by a matrix of social, cultural and historical contexts. These include the sociocultural environment in which the text was produced, the sociocultural circumstances of the child who is reading the text, where it is being read, and with whom. 'At any given time, in any given place, there will be a set of conditions … that will ensure that a word uttered in that place will have a meaning different than it would have had under any other conditions.'[22]

This perspective supports the argument that readers 'mispreread' texts, shaping the words they read to fit prior assumptions about the world and the literature they are reading.[23] In Bakhtin's scheme, however, the interplay of text and context, reader and text, self and other, is mutually transformative and inexhaustible. Bakhtin argues that meaning is something we rent from other consciousnesses (texts included).[24] This is an ongoing process with no definitive, conclusive outcomes. As far as meaningful engagement with literary texts is concerned, the process begins in infancy – with the help of an adult co-reader (see the discussion of book-reading routines above) – and continues in partnership with the text itself. In both cases, reading is a creative, transformative event for the participants in the dialogical exchange.

4.3 Word and image: reading multimodal texts

The first texts children encounter are usually picturebooks – books that require young readers to negotiate the meanings of words and pictures in complex ways. In a picturebook, the words and images are interdependent. Words are brought to life by the pictures, and the pictures live through the words. At times it is almost as if the words are being 'pulled through the pictures,'[25] so intimate is their connection.

The interrelationship of word and image can take a number of forms:

- **Congruence**: words and pictures tell essentially the same story, but the pictures always extend the text in some way.
- **Enhancement or augmentation**: picturing figurative language, for example, or transforming literal text into visual metaphor.
- **Deviation**: words and images tell different (parallel) stories or even contradict one another.

Dissonance between word and image may be exploited for different effects. 'The Hungry Three' series by Russell Hoban and Colin McNaughton features the make-believe adventures of three brothers who face various 'shock horrors' in the wilds of Backgar Den. The illustrations challenge much of what is said in the written text, creating lively narratives which are infused with alliterative wordplay, exotic place names and snippets of invented language. In *The Flight of Bembel Rudzuk*, the wizard Bembel Rudzuk (brother number one) creates a giant squidgerino squelcher (a length of twisted sheeting and a dripping sponge propelled by brothers one and two). The squidgerino squelcher slops and slithers, slobbers and moans as it makes its loathsome way across the kitchen floor, much to the dismay of the princess unguarded. 'Where'd this monster come from? And who's going to clean up after it?' she warns as she retrieves her cloak of darkness and shopping basket, and is gone with a 'whoosh!' Ultimately, the pleasure of the text lies in the playful dialogue between the illustrations and the written text. Theirs is an ambiguous, nuanced relationship which is handled with a light touch.

Picturebooks are multimodal texts, combining as they usually do two semiotic (meaning-making) modes or systems: linguistic discourse and visual representation.[26] To make sense of the narrative, readers interact with the words (which are usually written sequentially and in accordance with a host of linguistic rules) and the images (which have their own elaborate 'visual grammar'[27]). Significant visual codes include color, mood, shape, line, composition, framing, style, cultural references and visual symbolism. (See Chapter 6 – 'Orientation: textual features' – for further details.)

Régis Faller's *Polo: The Runaway Book* is a graphic novel which foregrounds, and plays on, the codes which constitute the grammar of visual images, particularly the codes of color, line and movement. The game begins in the peritext, where the back story is told in panels on a brilliant red background. Rabbit buys a book for her friend Polo, a small dog with a quizzical face. The book shop is conveniently located in a teapot and puffs of steam drift across a midnight sky and on beyond the right hand margin. The radiant images in these first frames represent a study in color (and, by extension, a study in hues, intensity, brightness, tints and shades), with at least three shades of red (scarlet, maroon and burgundy) offset by canary yellow, pure white and pitch black.

Moving to the story proper, the mood intensifies. We see Polo reading his new book in his bedroom deep within a tree. His book-filled room, which occupies the entire page, is illuminated by a glowing night-light which floods the space with color (purples, greens, yellows and blues), creating an idyllic world. While Polo sleeps, a long thread unfurls outside his window and a tiny fluorescent creature slips in and steals his book. 'My book!' he cries and just has time to grasp the line still dangling through the window.

Like Harold with his purple pencil,[28] Polo follows the line as the sky opens up before him, subtle shades of blue upon blue darkening as he climbs. In the course of the journey, the line transforms into a series of footprints, an unravelling skein of wool, a desert city with palm trees, a castle, an airship, a jungle vine, a rope ladder, a glider, a bean stalk, a drawbridge, and a steering wheel: all refuges and means of transport which advance his quest. The steady sense of momentum is reinforced by the fact that each panel replicates at least one element from the preceding frame: a clever strategy which contributes to the structural unity of the work.

Picturebooks may also challenge preconceptions about what actually constitutes visual representation. *Meow Ruff* by Joyce Sidman and Michelle Berg is a case in point. From its onomatopoeic title to the definition of concrete poetry hidden on the back cover ('CONCRETE POETRY IS POETRY THAT MAKES PICTURES OUT OF LETTERS AND WORDS' read the grassy letters, their tips breaking through the stretch of lawn which grows along the margin), *Meow Ruff* offers young readers a different way of interacting with written text and visual imagery. In the world of *Meow Ruff*, everything in the story, including the clouds and the raindrops, the footpath and the picnic bench, is a character with its own distinctive voice.[29] We will see this tendency in playful texts by writers such as the Ahlbergs, Anthony Browne and Russell Hoban – texts which highlight unusual perspectives and the secret lives of things – but *Meow Ruff* is exceptional in the way it portrays these elements in word-pictures. The story centers on a dog and a cat who fight then make peace. As the narrative unfolds, the cat-text shrieks 'back arching – hiss starting – sworn enemy – DOG!' when it is confronted by the dog's frenzied 'catcatcatcatcat!' A flock of crows comments on the action: 'fur will fly!' and 'dog in tree?' while lady bugs take flight ('really beetles,' they inform us, 'and not all ladies') and ants seek shelter: 'march march march'. In this way the text offers its readers lessons in poetics (personification, onomatopoeia, metaphor, repetition, rhythm and rhyme), punctuation (through the use of ellipses, dashes, exclamations, questions and quotation marks) and sensory image making: 'SUNWARMED, APPLE-CLOVER, SHOES-OFF, LEAF-GREEN, DEW-SOFTENED GRASS.'

The poetry, presented in block text, sits within colorful pictures of the characters it represents. Here is a car in a driveway:

SILVER-GLINTING
CHROME-PLATED
MANY-WINDOWED
HUMMING MACHINE
ROLLS TO A STOP

and an aged tree:

EACH LEAF
A MAP OF
BRANCHES
EACH TWIG
A BRANCH
OF LEAVES
EACH BRANCH
A TREE OF TWIGS
EACH TREE
A GREEN
HAIRED

SLIM
CHESTED
GREAT HEARTED
GNARL-ARMED
STRONG
LEGGED
DEEP-ROOTED
ONE

All images are multidimensional. Artists have traditionally used three dimensions of illustrative space (foreground, middle ground and background) to create vector-connections, perspective and point of view. Some innovative picturebooks go further, however, manipulating story space in surprising ways. As discussed by Bette Goldstone, these texts frequently exploit the space that exists between the reading/viewing audience and the book itself. [30] The picturebooks I have in mind take pleasure in transgressing this space: characters move in and out of the reader's domain, addressing the reader, discussing other characters and elements of the narrative, tinkering with title pages and publishers' details, and generally drawing attention to the status of the text as a work of fiction in the hands of a reader. Jack, the narrator of Scieszka and Smith's *The Stinky Cheese Man and Other Fairly Stupid Tales*, shows us how it is done:

Figure 10 From *The Stinky Cheese Man and Other Fairly Stupid Tales* by Jon Scieszka and Lane Smith

From time to time, picturebooks also allow readers (and characters) to venture deep into the third dimension of story space, the territory that lies *beneath* or *within* the actual, printed page. When Morris, the central character in *The Fantastic Flying Books of Mr. Morris Lessmore* by William Joyce, becomes lost in a book he literally slips through the pages, tripping over serifs, breaking his fall on a giant letter J, and skittering along a line of prose, scattering letters in his wake. This is impressive, but when David Wiesner's three pigs fold their page into a paper plane and fly right out of the story, they take narrative boundary breaking to a new level.

Figure 11 From *The Three Pigs* by David Wiesner

The multidimensional realm of story space serves another important function. It is the place where we find the nested stories within stories that figure in so many metafictive texts. There is, of course, one particular context in which children are increasingly likely to encounter embedded texts layered one on top of the other: in the digital space of hypertext. There, children can follow links, navigate in and out of websites, manipulate multiple images, make online connections, and journey through cyberspace. These digital interactions represent diverse reading experiences and may well affect the ways in which children respond to words and images on the printed page. We are still learning about the influence of touch-screen/ online interactions, and this will be a critical area of research for years to come.

There are many other ways that picturebooks can test the boundaries of meaning-making. Traditional stories can morph into mashups (as in Scieszka and Smith's *Squids will be Squids: Fresh Morals, Beastly Tales*); the distinctions between words and images can fade or disappear (as we've seen in *Meow Ruff*); and readers can find themselves in ontologically challenging territory (Art Spiegelman's *Open Me ... I'm a Dog!*). Texts such as these do not unfold in a linear manner: readers don't just read on to find out what happens next. Readers must negotiate different dimensions of story space and story time to make the connections required by the narrative.

In the next chapter I will show how playful texts and metafictions support young readers in this amazing process.

Notes

1 Lauren Child, *Who's Afraid of the Big Bad Book* (London: Hodder Children's Books, 2002; New York: Disney-Hyperion, 2003), unnumbered pages 6 and 7.
2 Margaret Meek, *How Texts Teach What Readers Learn* (Stroud, UK: The Thimble Press, 1988), 10.
3 Jerome S. Bruner, *Actual Minds, Possible Worlds* (Cambridge MA: Harvard University Press, 1986), 77.

   Jerome Bruner draws substantially on Vygotsky's ideas about the 'zone of proximal development'. Vygotsky defines the zone of proximal development as 'the distance between the actual development level as determined by independent problem solving and the level of potential development as determined through problem solving under adult guidance or in collaboration with more capable peers'. See L. S. Vygotsky's *Mind in Society: The Development of Higher Psychological Processes*, eds. M. Cole, V. John-Steiner, S. Scribner and E. Souberman (Cambridge, MA: Harvard University Press, 1978), 86. For an overview of Vygotsky's theory of transactional learning see Jerome S. Bruner, 'Vygotsky: a historical and conceptual perspective', in *Culture, Communication and Cognition: Vygotskian Perspectives*, 21–34.
4 J. A. Appleyard, *Becoming a Reader: The Experience of Fiction from Childhood to Adulthood* (New York: Cambridge University Press, 1994), 49.
5 See the detailed accounts in Shelby Anne Wolf and Shirley Brice Heath, *The Braid of Literature: Children's Worlds of Reading* (Cambridge MA: Harvard University Press, 1992).
6 Ibid., 130, 135.
7 Meek, *How Texts Teach*, 13.
8 Pat Hutchins, *Rosie's Walk* (London: The Bodley Head, 1968; New York: Simon and Schuster, 1968).
9 Meek, *How Texts Teach*, 13.
10 Wolfgang Iser, *The Act of Reading: A Theory of Aesthetic Response* (Baltimore, MD: Johns Hopkins University Press, 1978) and 'The reading process: a phenomenological approach', in *Reader Response Criticism: From Formalism to Post-Structuralism*, ed. Jane P. Tompkins (Baltimore, MD: Johns Hopkins University Press, 1980), 50–69.
11 Iser, *The Act of Reading*, 61. According to Iser, the text actually constructs a hypothetical, implied reader – a concept which is in no way to be identified with

any real reader – who 'prestructures the role to be assumed by each recipient' (p. 34) and functions as a guide to how the text can be read. The distinction between real and implied reader has been the subject of considerable debate among children's literature critics. I support Aidan Chambers' conceptualization of the implied reader as the 'the reader's second self – the reader-in-the-book – [who] is given certain attributes, a certain persona, created by the techniques and devices which help form the narrative. And this persona is guided by the author towards the book's potential meanings.' See Aidan Chambers, 'The reader in the book', in *Booktalk: Occasional Writing on Literature and Children* (London: Bodley Head, 1985; Woodchester: The Thimble Press, 1995), 36.

12 Iser, 'The reading process: A phenomenological approach', 51.

13 Iser, *The Act of Reading*, 68.

14 Ibid., 24.

15 Roland Barthes, *Image, Music, Text*, trans. Stephen Heath (New York: The Noonday Press, 1977), 157, 162–163.

16 For more on this point, see Louise M. Rosenblatt, *The Reader, the Text, the Poem: The Transactional Theory of the Literary Work* (Carbondale, IL: Southern Illinois University Press, 1978), 29: '[the] concept of transaction emphasizes the relationship with, *and continuing awareness of,* the text.'

17 Meek, *How Texts Teach*, 25. The notion of dialogicality derives from Mikhail Bakhtin's landmark study, *The Dialogic Imagination*. See M. M. Bakhtin, *The Dialogic Imagination: Four Essays*, ed. Michael Holquist, trans. Caryl Emerson and Michael Holquist (Austin, TX: University of Texas Press, 1981).

18 The structuring force which enables these connections to be made Bakhtin describes as 'architectonics'. For more on this intriguing subject, see Katerina Clark and Michael Holquist, *Mikhail Bakhtin* (Cambridge MA: Harvard University Press, 1984), 83–84.

19 I will return to this theme in some detail in my discussion of *The Mouse and His Child* and other multidimensional texts in Chapter 5.

20 Cited by David Crystal in *Language Play* (Harmondsworth: Penguin Books, 1998), 166.

21 Intertextuality is an extension of Bakhtinian dialogics. According to Julia Kristeva, who coined the term, 'any text is constructed as a mosaic of quotations' and 'any text is the absorption and transformation of another.' Julia Kristeva, 'Word, dialogue and novel', in *The Kristeva Reader*, ed. Toril Moi (Oxford: Blackwell, 1993), 37.

22 M. M. Bakhtin, *The Dialogic Imagination: Four Essays*, ed. Michael Holquist, trans. Caryl Emerson and Michael Holquist (Austin, TX: University of Texas Press, 1981), 428 (the glossary). Holquist is referring to the set of conditions defined by Bakhtin as 'heteroglossia'.

23 See Stanley Fish, *Is There a Text in This Class? The Authority of Interpretive Communities* (Cambridge MA: Harvard University Press, 1980), 311, cited in Roderick McGillis, *The Nimble Reader: Literary Theory and Children's Literature* (New York: Twayne Publishers, 1996), 16. As developing readers, children mispreread texts all the time.

24 McGillis, *The Nimble Reader*, 12. This view is similar in many ways to that of Vygotsky, Bruner and other theorists who have examined the scaffolding processes involved in the development of communication skills, reading abilities and the making of meaning in collaboration with others.

25 Margaret Meek, 'Children reading – now' in *After Alice: Exploring Children's Literature*, eds. Morag Styles, Eve Bearne and Victor Watson (London: Cassell, 1992), 176. Cited by David Lewis in *Reading Contemporary Picturebooks: Picturing Text* (London: Routledge/Falmer, 2001), 35.

26 Picturebooks can also be wordless, visual texts.

    'There are five semiotic systems in total: (1) Linguistic: comprising aspects such as vocabulary, generic structure and the grammar of oral and written language; (2) Visual: comprising aspects such as colour, vectors and viewpoint in still and moving images; (3) Audio: comprising aspects such as volume, pitch and rhythm of music and sound effects; (4) Gestural: comprising aspects such as movement, speed and stillness in facial expression and body language; (5) Spatial: comprising aspects such as proximity, direction, position of layout and organisation in space.' This summary is from Michele Anstey and Geoff Bull, 'Helping teachers explore multimodal texts', *Curriculum Leadership* (now *Curriculum and Leadership Journal*) 8(16) (4 June 2010), retrieved on 28 June 2014 from www.curriculum.edu.au/leader/helping_teachers_to_explore_multimodal_texts,31522.html?issueID=12207. Key studies of multimodal discourse include G. Kress and T. van Leeuwen, *Multimodal Discourse* (London: Arnold, 2001) and G. Kress, *Literacy in the New Media Age* (London: Routledge, 2003).

27 As defined by G. Kress and T. van Leeuwen in *Reading Images: A Grammar of Visual Design* (London: Routledge, 1996), and as discussed by David Lewis in *Reading Contemporary Picturebooks*, especially 102–123.

28 I discuss Crockett Johnson's classic text in Chapter 5.

29 Joyce Sidman writes: 'This book ... was a combination of my two greatest poetry loves: concrete poetry ... and "mask" poetry (in which you pretend to be something else and speak with its voice.)' Retrieved on 28 June 2014 from www.joycesidman.com/books

30 Bette Goldstone, 'The paradox of space in postmodern picturebooks', in *Postmodern Picturebooks: Play, Parody and Self-Referentiality*, eds. Lawrence R. Sipe and Sylvia Pantaleo (New York: Routledge, 2008), 117–129.

5 Playful texts

When the saleslady wound the key in the mouse father's back he
danced in a circle, swinging his little son up off the counter and
down again while the children laughed and reached out to touch
them. Around and around they danced gravely, and more and more
slowly as the spring unwound, until the mouse father came to a
stop holding the child high in his upraised arms.

Russell Hoban, The Mouse and His Child[1]

5.1 Playbooks and puzzles

Playbooks for children have a long history. Playful elements in English-
language texts began to emerge in the eighteenth century. Books such as *A
Playbook for Children to Allure Them to Read as Soon as They Can Speak
Plain* by 'J.G.' (1694) and *A Little Pretty Pocket Book* (published by John
Newbery in 1744), while decidedly moralistic, marked a shift in attitudes to
reading instruction. The dreary primers commonly used in nurseries and
classrooms gave way to more light-hearted fare which focused on the won-
ders of the natural world and incorporated engaging illustrations, games
and puzzles. Innovations in publishing for educational purposes produced
increasingly elaborate playforms such as harlequinades (lift-the-flap narratives which mimic the changing scenes in pantomime productions), pop-
ups, *volvelles* (paper constructions with rotating parts), miniature books
and micrographia.

Concurrently, literary texts for children became much more entertaining. As the idea that children's books could be both amusing and instructive
gained acceptance, more books were published. In Europe, landmarks included *Struwwelpeter* in 1845 and *Max and Moritz* in 1865. Joel Chandler's
trickster, Brer Rabbit, made his appearance in the United States in 1880,

and the first of the classic Australian *Cole's Funny Picture Book* series was published in 1879.

Nonsense, which emerged as a form of entertainment for children in nursery rhymes and collections of folk and fairy tales, came into its own with the *Alice* books and Edward Lear's nonsense miscellanies. On reflection, however, it is possible to discern a nonsensical, carnivalesque quality in many early children's books: even a work as didactic as Charles Kingsley's *The Water Babies*, the first English-language fantasy novel for children, demonstrates with its obsessive list making and its formal inversions, reversals, logical absurdities and intertextual allusions many of the defining features of nonsense.

Literary texts for children may exploit the possibilities of play in a variety of ways. Toy books which invite curious readers to spin dials, lift flaps, peer through cut-outs or miniature lenses, and make sense of 'fragments of text which must be physically lifted out of the fabric of the book itself and unfolded in order to be read'[2] represent variations on the playbook theme.

An outstanding movable book dating from 1929 and still in print is Tom (Martha) Seidmann-Freud's *The Magic Boat (Das Zauberboot)*. This marvellous little volume exemplifies the toy book genre. Designed to 'delight and surprise', it is a compendium of poems, original stories, folk tales and interactive games, including a Punch and Judy puppet show with parts for all players. The stylized illustrations feature tabs, wheels, grids and templates, creating multiple storylines and shifting perspectives.

Thanks to advances in printing and production techniques, movable books have become much more complex in the past 30 years or so, incorporating fantastic mechanical devices and feats of paper engineering. Leading figures in pop-up design such as David A. Carter and Jan Pieńkowski (*Haunted House, Robot*) are acclaimed for their engaging interactive texts. *One Red Dot*, the first in David Carter's 'Red Dot' series, celebrates the playful moods and vibrant colors of abstract art with 10 paper sculptures, each one paying tribute to a different geometric form (including a cube, cones and spirals, 'obedient orbs' and 'wiggle-wobble widgets'). The challenge for the reader is to find the single red dot hidden in each sculpture. *600 Black Spots* takes the conceit even further, offering towers of paper and floating arrays of black dots, threaded, coiled and suspended in fragile but incredibly flexible structures.

Texts which challenge the two-dimensional nature of the printed page in this way – drawing attention to their status as constructed objects – may also qualify as metafictions. I will have more to say about playful metafictions shortly.

Many playbooks feature toys as characters or, more specifically, toy characters which come alive.[3] The list is too extensive to cover comprehensively, but a representative selection might include 'Nutcracker and the King of Mice,' 'The steadfast tin soldier,' *Pinocchio, Winnie-the Pooh, The Midnight Folk, The Velveteen Rabbit, The Doll's House, The Mouse and His Child*, Lynne Reid Banks's *The Indian in the Cupboard*, and, for older readers, Neil Gaiman's eerie *Coraline*.

Russell Hoban and Nicola Bayley's collection of connected stories, *La Corona and the Tin Frog*, recasts the toy narrative in an enigmatic manner. The heroine of the story which gives the collection its name is trapped inside the decorative lid of a cigar box, frozen in time, while a dozen or more possible worlds hover just beyond her gaze. La Corona presides over an enchanted domain. With its lustrous colors and burnished tones, its symbolism (anvil, scythe and broken pillar, a sheath of wheat and a golden globe) and its emblems of discovery and exploration (a paddle steamer, a steam train and a hot air balloon floating above the horizon), the scene shimmers with expectation.

Inside the box live a seashell, a yellow tape measure, a magnifying glass, and a tin frog who has fallen in love with La Corona. At the transitional moment between midnight and the 12 strokes of the clock, the companions plunge down deep into the luminous image on the cigar box lid. The colored dots which constitute the picture close behind them and they find themselves in the painting with La Corona, together at last.

Other playbooks incorporate puzzles and tests of various kinds. On one level, all picturebooks can be read in this light. In order to make sense of the narrative, the reader must solve the puzzle of the story the images imply.[4] There are numerous texts, however, which make explicit use of puzzles as a play device. Model texts include Graeme Base's *The Eleventh Hour*, which includes a decryption code for detective readers, David Legge's *Bamboozled*, which creates a nonsensical topsy-turvy world for its readers to explore, and Rosenthal and Lichtenheld's *Duck! Rabbit!*, introduced in Chapter 2.

Mazes, lookalikes, spot-the-differences, armchair treasure hunts, and the many versions of *Where's Wally?* all fall into the puzzle book category. So do alphabet puzzles, which are so numerous and diverse they really constitute a subgenre of their own.

Alphabet puzzles are significant for a number of reasons. Since they play with language and interrogate the rules of linguistic discourse (specifically, the rules of alphabetical order), they serve a metalinguistic function and are allied to literary nonsense. They are extremely adaptable, readily transforming into jigsaw puzzles and online games. They can also be manipulated in diverse ways without compromising their linguistic integrity. *Anno's Magical ABC* highlights the possibilities of the genre in an original way. The book, which can be read front to back or back to front, comprises a series of 'anamorphic' letters and associated images which have been tightly compressed and then stretched out like plasticine. The best way to read the alphabet is with the curved silver mirror which comes with the book.

Texts may also portray or re-enact play for different purposes. In Allan Baillie and Jane Tanner's *Drac and the Gremlin*, for instance, the concept of cooperative play between siblings is presently in an idealized manner. Other books inscribe particular games such as 'I spy' (Janet and Allan Ahlberg's *Each Peach Pear Plum*) or peekaboo. (There are scores of examples of peekaboo play. Two of the very best are the Ahlbergs' *Peepo!* and *Anno's Peekaboo*, cited in Chapter 2 and discussed in more detail later in this chapter). For slapstick humor and great comic timing it is hard to go past Colin McNaughton's picturebook series featuring Preston Pig (including *Suddenly!*, *Boo!*, *Oops!* and *Oomph!*).

Children's novels can also celebrate the pleasures of make-believe sociodramatic play. Books for older readers typically take the form of adventure stories or stories of suspense. The greatest of these belong to another era: E. Nesbit's *The Story of the Treasure Seekers* was published in 1899, and the first novel in Arthur Ransome's *Swallows and Amazons* series appeared in 1930.

The *Swallows and Amazons* stories, with their intertextual references to *Treasure Island* and *Robinson Crusoe*, are based on sustained episodes of pretend play. Characters explore deserted islands, trek to the North Pole in the deepest Arctic winter, and brave the perilous waters of the North Sea, assuming pirate personae and engaging in lots of serious swashbuckling. The novels are remarkable in many ways. They are firmly grounded in real life – *Swallows and Amazons* doubles as a handbook of outdoor survival skills, with detailed instructions for trimming lanterns, tying knots and setting sails – and yet they constitute entirely convincing portrayals of collaborative pretend play. Fortunately, the works of Arthur Ransome and E. Nesbit remain in print and are still readily available.

Books which take a more interrogative approach to play include John Burningham's picturebooks: *Come Away from the Water, Shirley* and *Time to Get Out of the Bath, Shirley*. These profoundly imaginative stories are told from two contrasting perspectives. While Shirley's parents, who are depicted in delicate line drawings, worry about her making a mess in the bathroom or befriending stray dogs at the beach, Shirley creates dazzling make-believe worlds, where she sails with pirates and duels with knights on horseback. The counterpoint of word and image, and the simultaneous unfolding of two very different modes of narration, is achieved with great elegance. 'The surprise for the reader, and the reading lesson, lies in the discovery of the two kinds of storytelling side by side.'[5]

While all of the texts discussed so far in this chapter highlight the *operations* of play, they are not necessarily 'playful texts' in the sense that I use the term in this book. It is time to address this central issue.

5.2 Metafictive playfulness: some models and definitions

To be considered playful, a text must play on words and/or images in the same way that children play in games of make-believe, transforming the everyday world of common sense meaning into a self-reflexive playworld which works to disclose, and subvert, the rules which sustain it. Playful narrative turns back on itself, reflexively, like an image reflected in a mirror,[6] to reveal the terms of its making.[7] This is undoubtedly one of the reasons why mirror images, stories within stories, and dreams within dreams figure so prominently in nonsense texts and other playful metafictions.

Playful texts use many different devices to disrupt our expectations. In the same way that make-believe play depends on the ability to step outside oneself and take on other roles, playful texts ask the reader to participate in a process of contextual reframing (such as that conveyed by the message 'this is play') accompanied by the subversion of conventional narrative practices. As we will see later in this chapter, techniques employed to effect this transformation within the text include play with modes of discourse (especially linguistic and pictorial discourse) and play with the conventions of storytelling (including modes and levels of narration).

Strategies such as these serve to draw attention to the fictional nature of texts. This self-conscious textuality is not new. Pop-up books, which challenge our notions of what a book might be, were popular in the eighteenth and nineteenth centuries, and the Alice books, with their peculiarly Victorian sensibility, are thoroughly metafictive. The metafictive picturebook, however, really comes into its own with the publication of Winsor McCay's *Little Nemo in Slumberland* and Tove Jansson's early comics and picturebooks.

As Philip Nel has observed, *Little Nemo in Slumberland* is a metafictive triumph.[8] The *Little Nemo* comic strips appeared in the *New York Herald* and in William Randolph Hearst's *New York American* newspapers from 1905 to 1914 and 1924 to 1927.

Figure 12 From *Little Nemo in Slumberland* by Winsor McCay

McCay experimented with the comic strip form, manipulating the size and shape of panels and playing with perspective, dimension and framing. His dreamscapes are astonishing in scope and design. Intertextual (combining elements of baroque art with avant-garde expressionism and art nouveau), innovative, and infinitely strange, *Little Nemo in Slumberland* is a masterpiece of graphic design.

Tove Jansson's metafictive tour de force, *The Book about Moomin, Mymble and Little My*, was published in 1952. The metanarrative unfolds on four levels.

First of all, *The Book about Moomin, Mymble and Little My* is a **book** with heft and substance. It revels in its bookish components, giving them lots of work to do. It has a bold, inviting **cover** with a cut-away porthole on the front and a tiny see-through keyhole at the back. Both are important. The porthole is the reader's only way into the world of Moomin, Mymble and Mymble's sister, Little My, who has disappeared. The keyhole through the back cover is small enough to keep the characters inside the book, but large enough to allow readers to peek out and see another world waiting beyond the story. The **pages** of the book feature intricate cut-outs which slice through multiple layers and remind us what pages are for. As we read on with Moomin and Mymble, we can look for clues on the page, turn back to see things from other points of view, and use all of this information to infer what might happen next.

Second, this is a **publication**: we actually see the printer at work with tape and scissors and learn that 'The holes are cut at Schildts' (Jansson's publisher in Helsinki).

Next, we note that this is a **narrative**, a story told in words and images. The slices and excisions are a vital part of the narrative, serving as windows, doorways, caves, passageways and chambers through which the characters must pass. They create a sightline through the dense forest and, when the quest has been accomplished, open out onto the meadows of Moominvalley in spring. Significantly, the cut-outs highlight small details which prove to be critical as the story proceeds. They also reveal surprising connections between the eccentric inhabitants of Moominvalley: unruly Little My and the timid Fillyjonk, an obsessive Hemulen and the strange little Hattifatteners, who have no opinions about anything at all, but are attracted to lightning and are dangerous to touch.

Finally, *The Book about Moomin* is a **metanarrative** which draws attention to the status of the text as text and enables the reader to experience multiple dimensions of story space. In the double-page spread reproduced below, Moomin, Mymble and Little My have just jumped through a window and are falling into the Fillyjonk's bedroom. The representation of visual space is extraordinary: Mymble flies through the air (we can see rolling hills and Moomin's house far away in the background) as Moomin and Little My touch down. Backdrop and bedroom blend into one. The Fillyjonk is flattened. Terrified, she hurls herself through the next page, leaving a gaping hole as she flees, shrieking, into the distance. Here is the text which accompanies the action:

> They landed – it was quite amusing – where a fillyjonk was snoozing. 'Oh look,' said My. 'What's this red mat?' 'It's Fillyjonk! You've squashed her flat!' cried Mymble. 'Look, she's in a rage.' Fillyjonk howled and split this page. 'I think the fillyjonk escaped here, through this fillyjonkly-shaped hole,' Mymble said. 'This was her route.' So they set off in hot pursuit to where a new adventure beckoned. NOW GUESS WHAT HAPPENS IN A SECOND.[9]

In an odd, interactive aside, readers are also offered a small white scroll and are invited to draw the poor Fillyjonk once she's had time to compose herself. We needn't worry too much about this because the Fillyjonk, like all Tove Jansson's characters, is exceptionally resilient.

Figure 13 From *The Book about Moomin, Mymble and Little My* by Tove Jansson

The 1950s saw the publication of another landmark work of metafiction, this time drawn in 'metapictures'. I am referring to Crockett Johnson's *Harold and the Purple Crayon*, the perfectly simple story of a little boy who decided to go for a walk in the moonlight. Since he needed a moon, Harold took his purple crayon and drew one.

Figure 14 From *Harold and the Purple Crayon* by Crockett Johnson.

Then he set off, taking his crayon with him. He drew a forest and an apple tree with a dragon to guard it. He drew a boat and set sail on the ocean. Harold landed on a beach, drew an enormous picnic, and then drew a moose and a porcupine to help him finish it. He drew a mountain, a hot air balloon, a city full of windows, and a policeman to guide him. Then Harold drew his way home to bed.

This quiet story is clearly metafictive – Harold creates his own story in metapictures, with 'pictures that reflect on the nature of pictures and invite us to do so'[10] as well. *Harold and the Purple Crayon* is also a meditation on the nature of make-believe play. Harold draws in three dimensions and his drawings come alive; every stroke of his crayon conveys the message 'this is play'. Within his circumscribed playworld Harold is free to summon dragons, climb mountains, and draw himself in and out of danger. Throughout his journey he deals, playfully, with things as they exist and do not exist at the same time.

Little Nemo, The Book about Moomin, Mymble and Little My, and *Harold and the Purple Crayon* stand as models of metafictive playfulness. They have been enormously influential, as will become obvious in my discussion of contemporary texts. In the following pages I consider some of the finest examples of playful metafiction published in the past 60 years.

Since I hope that children will actually read these books, I have focused on texts which are either in print or are likely to be held by libraries.

All of these texts make demands of their readers, but there is nothing underhand about the way they go about this. Playful metafiction flaunts its fictional status, signaling 'this is fiction, this is play' clearly and systematically, inviting young readers who are prepared to play the game to become co-creators of the story world. This playful contract is modeled on the type of negotiations that take place when players engage in make-believe play. As discussed in Chapter 2, players need techniques for sustaining pretense and negotiating the content and conduct of pretend play. In theory, these negotiations can either take the form of out-of-frame metacommunication or within-frame play acting. In practice, however, the levels tend to become intertwined in such a way that all of the devices deployed to initiate change and coordinate meaning can be said to be metacommunicative – it is simply that some are more overtly so than others.

Apart from direct proposals to change roles or introduce new elements into the play script as the game proceeds ('let's say,' or 'pretend that'), one of the most common devices used to clarify and coordinate meaning in make-believe play is that of *underscoring*.[11] This option allows players to define their intention verbally while enacting it nonverbally ('I'm calling grandma' accompanied by the appropriate gestures). By highlighting the obvious in this way, underscoring tends to expose the playframe more than other forms of playful metacommunication.[12] While this might be expected to diminish the play experience, the opposite appears to be the case.

> Underscoring allows players to stay emotionally within the play world while clarifying definitions. Although in real life this redundant verbalization would disrupt the experience of the event, in make-believe play the verbalization deepens it ... Further experience of the details is often more important in play than the professed point of the activity.[13]

Playful metafiction asks young readers to engage with the text in the same way that they do in other forms of collaborative make-believe play. Having signaled that 'this is play,' the text proceeds to lay down the rules of the game. Because it is metafictive, it insists on drawing attention to the devices of its own making, taking care to make the rules of the game as transparent as possible and to underscore any rule-breaking activity which violates narrative codes and conventions. Readers who choose to participate not only commit themselves to becoming role players (assuming the roles of characters, co-narrators and co-authors of the fictional, make-believe world), but they also commit to a process of learning to interrogate the rules of meaning-making in partnership with the text, its intertexts and other readers.

Playful metafiction uses a number of techniques to initiate, underscore and sustain the proposition that 'this is fiction, this is play.' Key metafictive strategies include:

- **Narrative frame breaking and embedding**. Metafiction often interrogates the causal, logical or linear relationships that exist between narrative events, characters and narrators, and between primary and secondary narratives.[14] Texts may engage in metalepsis, or narrative frame breaking, to highlight the conventions of storytelling and underscore different narrative levels.[15] Many also feature stories within stories and embedded texts which reflect on primary narratives in diverse ways.
- **Intertextuality and polyphony**. As we will see, playful texts like to quote, imitate, parody and pay homage to other texts. Intertextuality also supports multiple readings, with children gaining more from the texts when they return to them as more experienced readers.
- **Word games, nonsense and other linguistic and visual play-forms**. Taking their cues from children's language play and nonsense, playful texts revel in linguistic play, visual metaphors, and other symbolic forms of expression. Playful tropes such as the *mise en abyme* figure prominently.

Keeping this theoretical framework in mind, it is time to turn to the texts themselves. My discussion focuses on the ways in which the texts engage young readers in the meaning-making process. While this strategic approach may seem an odd way to tackle a subversive subject, I want to ensure that my analysis is as transparent and accessible as possible.

5.3 Textual play

Narrative frame breaking and embedding

Playful metafiction enjoys disrupting narrative conventions. It takes every opportunity to caricature traditional genres and retell familiar stories from different perspectives. In the world of fractured fairy tales, revisionism rules. The ugly duckling grows up to be an ugly duck (as it does in *The*

Stinky Cheese Man); Cinderella escapes from a demented prince (in Roald Dahl and Quentin Blake's *Revolting Rhymes*); and Goldilocks turns out to be a serial felon (in Lauren Child's *Who's Afraid of the Big Bad Book*).

The characters of Little Red Riding Hood and The Three Pigs are particularly irrepressible, their stories morphing into such wildly divergent versions as *The True Story of the Three Little Pigs* (by Jon Scieszka and Lane Smith), *The Three Little Wolves and the Big Bad Pig* (by Eugene Trivizas and Helen Oxenbury), *Anno's Three Little Pigs* (an elegant explanation of computer programming and mathematical problem solving), David Wiesner's *The Three Pigs* (discussed below), Roald Dahl's revolting 'Little Red Riding Hood and the Wolf', and most improbably, *Little Red Writing* (by Joan Holub and Melissa Sweet). In this latter version of the Red Riding Hood tale, Little Red, a glossy red pencil, sets out to write a story. Equipped with a basket of nouns to keep her on track, she overcomes a host of narrative pitfalls (including a 'bosky' forest of superfluous adjectives, a runaway truckload of adverbs and a pot of conjunction glue) to reach the climax: an encounter with the Wolf 3000 pencil sharpener, 'the grumpiest, growliest, grindingest pencil sharpener ever made!'

Playful texts often destabilize the levels of narration which shape the fictional world. Like Jack in *The Stinky Cheese Man*, narrators may address readers, sneak into the story, argue with characters, and look for ways to undermine their authors. Characters can also jump from story to story or from a story within a story into the main narrative. They can tinker with endpapers and publishing details, rewrite endings and generally function as co-authors of their own tales. Characters may also refer and/or appeal to their readers, allude to other fictional worlds, or, like the narrator in *The Book about Moomin, Mymble and Little My*, speculate about the real world that exists beyond the text.

David Wiesner's *The Three Pigs* makes the most of these possibilities. The story begins conventionally, with muted illustrations which closely resemble Walter Crane's woodcuts. Three pigs go out into the world to seek their fortunes. The first pig builds his house out of straw; the wolf blows it down and eats the pig up. Or so the fairy tale text would have us believe. At this point the text actually splits. The fairy tale text continues in an increasingly befuddled manner while the pig, blown out of that story, climbs out of the frame into a metafictive realm of stark, white space. Eventually the other pigs join him and together they reclaim the fairy tale, folding its pages (with the wolf still affixed) into a getaway plane.

The text transgresses a suite of narrative boundaries. The pigs try out different identities (traditional fairy tale characters, Little Golden Book piglets, and curious domestic pigs), befriend stray characters, and inhabit various forms of discourse (fairy tale, nursery rhyme, illustrated alphabet, surreal picturebook, and fantasy quest), continually challenging the limits of the 'real' world and the imaginary in the process.

At one point, the straw-house pig, his snout pressed hard up against the picture plane, stares out at us saying, 'I think ... someone's out there.' This is an arresting experience, made all the more unsettling by the focus, scale, and perspective of the image – the pig is enormous and he is only millimeters away.

At the end of the book, in a final metafictive maneuver, the pigs reassemble the scattered pages of their story, disposing of excess letters as they see fit. They can't locate the final 'e' or 'r' so they have to live happily 'ever aft'. For more on the story, and the ways in which young readers negotiate its complexities, see the case study in Chapter 6 ('First grade children read Wiesner's *The Three Pigs*').

Co-authorship also comes to the fore in a series of metafictive texts which take their inspiration from *Harold and the Purple Crayon*. Anthony Browne's *Bear Hunt*, Mélanie Watt's *Chester*, and Allan Ahlberg and Bruce Ingman's *The Pencil* all feature pen- or pencil-wielding protagonists (in *The Pencil*, the pencil *is* the protagonist) who create the discourse in collaboration with readers. This kind of active involvement also serves as a metaphor for the way readers make meaning out of texts.

In *Bear Hunt*, Bear takes his magic pencil and goes for a walk in a psychedelic jungle. Unfortunately, two hunters (identified by their pith helmets, colorful socks and prodigious moustaches) are out hunting and they spy Bear. The reader and the narrator join forces at this point, shouting a warning: 'Look out Bear!' Bear promptly steps out of the story onto a blank, white page, where he draws two pegs and a trip wire. Back in the jungle, a hunter falls flat on his face. The narrative proceeds in this manner, with the resourceful Bear continually drawing himself out of trouble. 'At every moment of crisis he appears to be able to slip out of the fictional world that Browne has created for him and into the realm more properly occupied by the author/illustrator, for it is the latter who actually creates the images that embody the fiction.'[16] To observe how children respond to this wonderful exercise in metalepsis, see the Williams and Jack study in Chapter 6 ('Abdullah and Mark: Learning to read with *Bear Hunt*').

In Ahlberg and Ingman's *The Pencil*, things get out of hand when an obliging pencil draws a little boy, whom he names Banjo. Banjo asks for a dog to keep him company, and the dog asks for a cat to chase. Then they need a house to live in, streets to run through, food to eat. Black-and-white food makes everyone depressed, so the pencil draws a paintbrush named Kitty who colors their world. The family grows and everyone begins to complain. 'This hat looks silly.' 'My ears are too big.' 'I shouldn't be smoking a pipe.' So the pencil creates a rubber ... and that's when the trouble really begins.

The Pencil sparkles with good humor. The illustrations are joyful and exceptionally engaging. You can, as one reviewer comments, 'almost feel the graphite moving sensuously across the textured paper.'[17] This is a story where every detail is closely observed and everything matters. The ants (Alice, Alvie, Abraham, Amy, Araminta, Alberic, Algernon, Anastasia, Ada and Allan) marching across the tablecloth matter, and so does the soccer ball:

> 'What's my name?' said the ball.
> 'Don't be silly,' said the pencil.
> The ball made a sad face.
> 'All right then "Sebastian,"' said
> the pencil.

Figure 15 From *The Pencil* by Allan Ahlberg and Bruce Ingman

Humor aside (and this is a very funny book), *The Pencil* reveals a preoccupation with the secret lives of things which is very similar to the tendency which we observed in *Meow Ruff* (see Chapter 4). It is, in fact, one of the defining features of playful metafiction. As I will show, playful texts which invite young readers to engage in hypothetical thinking, to look closely and make connections between *this* and *that*, tend to sustain multiple perspectives and support alternative points of view. It is a fascinating aspect of textual playfulness, and one that reinforces the links between playful metafiction and make-believe play.

Perspective taking is celebrated in another metafictive text: David Macaulay's *Black and White*. Part picturebook, part hypertext, *Black and White* resembles a web page with four discrete but ultimately connected stories laid out across each double-page spread. Readers may choose to pursue each individual storyline to its conclusion or to negotiate all four at once – a challenging but achievable task for children who are familiar with digital technologies. The text foregrounds its subversive intention when it pronounces at the beginning:

> WARNING
> This book contains a number of stories that do not necessarily occur at the same time. Then again, it may contain only one story. In any event, careful inspection of both words and pictures is recommended.[18]

This reading lesson is pasted across a black-and-white image of a prison cell. The bars have been shattered and a knotted length of cloth signals that an escape has recently taken place. When we turn the page we see the escapee, dressed in striped prison garb, climbing into his particular story. There are, as mentioned, four separate stories, each with its own title page and distinctive style of illustration.

As the liner notes tell us, there is a boy traveling home by train ('Seeing things'). There are some absent-minded parents who begin to act very strangely ('Problem Parents'). There are commuters waiting at a railway station ('A Waiting Game'). And there are the very many black-and-white figures (Holstein cows and other characters) which are on the loose and are almost impossible to identify ('Udder Chaos').

Each of the stories has its own narrator and its own unique tone. Attentive readers will find many clues to help them trace the complex pattern of interactions which ties the narratives together. Most of the clues are embedded in the visual discourse; the written text tends to be more inscrutable, but it does yield more with subsequent readings.[19] *Black and White* is an inexhaustible textual puzzle, best shared with other readers.

Playful texts can defy narrative conventions by offering devious narrators, by creating biographies of non-existent writers, or by presenting fictional works by imaginary characters and involving the author in the lives of those characters. Strategies such as these serve to interrogate the relationship between truth, fiction and reality.[20] Three important texts exemplify this phenomenon: Chris Van Allsburg's picturebook, *The Mysteries of Harris Burdick*, Geraldine McCaughrean's novel for older children, *A Pack of Lies: Twelve stories in one*, and Aidan Chambers' young adult novel, *Breaktime*, the first novel in the author's six volume 'Dance Sequence.'

The Mysteries of Harris Burdick consists of a series of 14 black-and-white drawings, each with a title and a short caption. In the frontispiece, Van Allsburg attributes the drawings to an elusive figure named Harris Burdick whom he has never met. Van Allsburg tells us only that he first saw Burdick's drawings at the house of the retired publisher, Peter Wenders (to whom the book is dedicated). According to Wenders, Harris Burdick had visited his office 30 years before and handed him a single illustration from each of the stories he hoped to have published. Wenders admired the drawings and asked to see the stories, but Burdick never returned. With Wenders's permission, Van Allsburg announces that he has decided to publish the portfolio so a new generation of readers will have the chance to complete the stories for themselves.

In its layering of fiction upon fiction, Harris Burdick deploys a narrative conceit with precedents in works of fiction such as *Don Quixote*, *Wuthering Heights*, and *The Narrative of Arthur Gordon Pym*,[21] texts which play with the effacement of the author and come wrapped in layers of prefatory material which make it almost impossible to tell where the peritext ends and the story proper begins.

Stepping over the threshold into the story itself, *The Mysteries of Harris Burdick* presents a series of intensely charged and super-realistic tableaux: some haunting, some idyllic, and all capturing the exact moment when the real world and the world of the imagination collide. These images and the cryptic captions which accompany them manage to convey many things: the claustrophobic effects of the supernatural, for example, where everything familiar turns in upon itself, acquiring new, sinister meanings in the process, and, at the other end of the spectrum, the playful implications of reverie, that liminal state which opens onto expansive imaginary landscapes where one can be completely oneself and outside oneself at the same time. For young readers, the mysteries of Harris Burdick offer a double challenge: the creation of meaning *and* story.

In Geraldine McCaughrean's metafictive novel, *A Pack of Lies: Twelve Stories in One*, the fictional lives of the characters who inhabit the different strands of the narrative become so inextricably interlinked that readers can easily lose track of their identities. *A Pack of Lies* is a collection of tall stories, each belonging to a different genre, and each providing a different perspective on the connections between truth and fiction, telling stories and telling lies. The most puzzling aspect of the collection, however, concerns its narrator, one MCC Berkshire, who comes from the English town of Reading. The homographic play on his home town (that's *Reading* to rhyme with 'bedding', not *Reading* to rhyme with 'breeding', as we're told in chapter 1) is the first of many clues to MCC's identity, but it's not until the last page that the mystery is solved – and even then it takes some working out.

While MCC Berkshire inhabits a metafictive world composed entirely of stories, Ditto, the attractive but unreliable narrator of Aidan Chambers's *Breaktime* exists in the abstract realm of metalanguage.

> Ditto's name signals that this is so. 'Ditto' means a repetition symbolized by two small marks ("). He is therefore, simply, a drawing, marks on a page, just as his story is nothing but writing. In a literal sense, all writing is drawing, having no reality except in the marks themselves. Thus Ditto is, as a ditto sign, a tautology, a self-sustaining being who exists only by indicating his own repetition.[22]

It should also be noted that in naming his character, Chambers pays homage to the masters of metalinguistic playfulness and reflexive thinking, Tweedledum and Tweedledee:

> 'If that there King was to wake,' added Tweedledum, 'you'd go out
> – bang! – just like a candle!'
> 'I shouldn't!' Alice exclaimed indignantly. 'Besides, if I'm only a sort
> of a thing in his dream, what are *you*, I should like to know?'
> 'Ditto,' said Tweedledum.
> 'Ditto, ditto!' said Tweedledee.[23]

Occasionally, characters exist in parallel fictional worlds. Lauren Child's character, Ruby Redfort, secret agent and ultra-cool narrator of the 'Ruby Redfort' series of novels[24] also appears in the author's *Clarice Bean* books, where she stars in the movie 'Run Ruby Run,' features in Clarice's much loved 'Ruby Redfort Collection' (titles include *There Was a Girl*

Called Ruby and *Are You for Real, Ruby Redfort?*), and dispenses practical advice in the *Ruby Redfort Spy Guide* and *Survival Handbook.*

Ruby Redfort makes metalepsis look easy – she moves effortlessly across genres and between levels of narration. While Ruby specializes in intratextual frame breaking, the characters in Philip Pullman's fairy tale, *Clockwork,* take an intertextual path.

Clockwork is an enigmatic concept, replete with playful potential. Hans Christian Andersen was captivated by the idea of windup mechanisms transforming inanimate objects into lifelike beings, and so was E. T. A. Hoffmann, whose influence Pullman specifically acknowledges. Intertextual allusions to Hoffman's masterpiece 'The Sandman' are to be found in the sinister figure of Dr (Coppelius) Kalmenius and, in a nod to Hoffmann via Freud, to the repeated descriptions of his dreadful craftsmanship as 'uncanny.'[25] While young readers will not catch many of these references, they highlight the polyphonic nature of the text and the fact that it will reward rereading. In Pullman's story, as in Russell Hoban's *The Mouse and His Child,* the clockwork trope also functions as a metaphor for the process of fiction-making, of fitting together all of the component parts to make the story run.

Clockwork offers the reader 'a story within a story and then another story within the first one.'[26] In the telling, diegetic levels converge in a way that enables the characters to jump from one level of narration to another. The interlocking stories tell of the dreadful fate that befalls Karl, an apprentice clockmaker who sells his soul to Dr Kalmenius; the prize won by Gretl, the innkeeper's daughter who rescues a prince with a clockwork heart; and the lesson learnt by Fritz, the hapless storyteller who, having wound up the stories and set them in motion, abandons his characters altogether.

Running parallel to these intersecting stories is another narrative discourse made up of a series of framed and illustrated captions. There the narrator reflects on the different strands of the narrative as they unfold, confiding in the reader and offering suggestions about possible ways of interpreting what is going on.

I will conclude this survey of metafictive frame breaking with three wordless texts composed entirely of embedded images and interwoven stories within stories.

The three texts in question, *Flotsam* by David Wiesner, *Zoom* by Istvan Banyai, and *The Red Book* by Barbara Lehman, invite us to gaze into the furthest reaches of story space, to discover worlds beyond the worlds imprinted on the page, and to see those worlds as others see them. Since this is a task requiring finely tuned perspective-taking skills, the texts supply a comprehensive selection of optical devices for the reader's use. *Flotsam* features at least five different kinds of lens (a magnifying glass, microscope, binoculars, camera, and multiple pairs of eyes), while *Zoom* and *The Red Book* 'fold into themselves'[27] like collapsible telescopes and make use of visual aids such as maps, screens and windows.

David Wiesner's *Flotsam* adopts an age-old storytelling structure: a frame story which contains a series of embedded stories within it. In this case, however, readers are presented with pictures within pictures, and with two parallel narratives, each of which has its own series of embeddings.

The frame story begins at the beach. A boy finds an old fashioned camera, eight shots to the roll, and he has the film developed. The eighth picture reveals the last child who held the camera (and all of the children before him, each one revealed as we zoom in to the power of 70x). The children are connected across time and space, their friendship sealed by the secret knowledge they share.[28] At the end of the story, the boy throws the camera back into the sea for another child to discover.

The second narrative reveals the camera's secret in a series of mesmerizing images – seven random glimpses of the worlds that exist beneath the sea and the mysterious lives that are lived there. One shot shows tropical fish welcoming a mechanical decoy to their school, another reveals giant starfish striding across the ocean floor with seashell islands clinging to their backs, and a third gives us an intimate portrait of an octopus family creating their living room from the contents of a submerged removals van. Invoking the spirit of Winsor McCay, these luminous dreamscapes celebrate the strangeness and the variety of life from multiple points of view.

Zoom and *The Red Book* play with viewpoint, scale and dimension in such a sustained and imaginative way that they constitute studies in perspective. The illustrations are perfect for this purpose. Both texts use strong color, minimal contrast, and *ligne claire* artwork[29] (where lines are drawn with equal weight and thickness) to take account of every detail and create a uniformly flat aspect which intensifies the playful approach to perspective which is taking place in the background and off the page.

Zoom is a reversible text which reads forwards and backwards. It begins with this cryptic image:

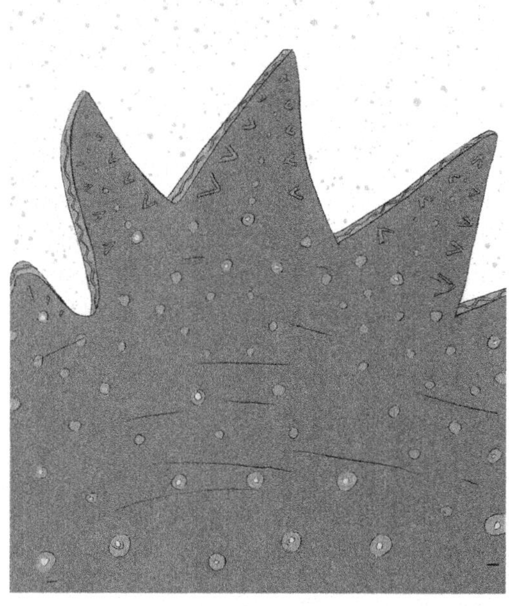

Figure 16 From *Zoom* by Istvan Banyai

Read on – zoom out – and a different picture emerges.

Figure 17 From *Zoom* by Istvan Banyai

Jig-saw children in a 3D farmhouse? The manipulation of perspective and dimension becomes increasingly complex as the images recede, frame by frame. Strangely, the illustrations also become more detailed as one moves away from them. Hands reach in to rearrange the pieces of a toy farm yard. Turn the page. A girl is playing with the pieces on a table. Pull back. She's on the cover of a toy catalogue ... resting in the lap of a boy who's fallen asleep ... on the deck of a cruise ship ... featured on a travel poster ... appearing in a TV advertisement screening in the Arizona desert ... which is reproduced on a postage stamp ... fixed to a letter ... delivered by an aircraft which flies on ... through the clouds ... beyond the earth ... into deepest space. Then repeat the process, back-to-front this time, to experience the sensation of 'falling through the pictures.'[30] (Refer to Chapter 6 – 'Engaging with wordless texts: children read *Zoom*' – to see how young readers respond to the text.)

The Red Book is another metafictive story about imaginary journeys, shared secrets and surprising connections. Two children, living in different parts of the world, become friends when they discover a magical book. The story is simple and the illustrations are exceptionally clear – so clear they are almost transparent. But readers need to look closely to see how astonishing these images really are. At critical moments in the narrative the pictures are superimposed in such a way that we can see *through* each image to the one underneath it. Consider the following double-page spread:

Figure 18 From *The Red Book* by Barbara Lehman

Having absorbed the little girl's portrait, the montage on the left folds her picture into a series of alternating images, each reflecting and complementing the other, as the children come face to face for the first time. The illustration captures a single moment, fixed in time, and suggests, simultaneously, a never-ending chain of encounters unfolding to infinity. This is a quintessential image for the digital age (with its succession of windows opening onto other windows) but more than that, it is a tribute to the power of the imagination, and to its pre-eminent medium: the book.

The interplay of illustrations in *The Red Book* is a fine example of mirror imagery, a device which is often employed by metafiction to highlight its self-reflexive nature. In its most extreme form – the *mise en abyme* – mirror imagery can be manipulated to replicate an entire text in miniature. I will examine this phenomenon in the next section.

Mirrors in the text: focus on the *mise en abyme*

The *mise en abyme* is one of the hallmarks of playful metafiction. It is a multimodal form (suited to verbal and visual representation) and it can serve both structural and thematic purposes. Like other types of make-believe play, it is self-contained but infinitely adaptable, circumscribed but conducive to hypothetical world-making.

The *mise en abyme* is a mirror-like reproduction of an image or text within itself.[31] It is a figurative device (or 'trope') which 'overturns' literal meaning, and it tends to have a special relationship with figures of speech such as metaphor, metonymy (substituting one concept with another, associated concept), and synecdoche (a particular kind of metonymy which occurs when part of a work reproduces the whole).

The *mise en abyme* incorporates unusual play strategies which readers are unlikely to encounter elsewhere. This is particularly noticeable in texts where *mises en abyme* are deployed to create a 'Chinese box' effect, suggesting an endless recession of internal duplications stretching to infinity. These texts invite readers to engage in the creation of alternative, make-believe worlds while experiencing the textual equivalent of *ilinx*,[32] that intoxicating form of play associated with carnival rides and the light-headed disorientation that they induce.

As is the case with all forms of play, the *mise en abyme* takes delight in design for its own sake. This is one of the characteristics which Anthony Browne exploits in *Through the Magic Mirror*:

Figure 19 From *Through the Magic Mirror* by Anthony Browne

The Ahlbergs approach the subject in a different way in the frontispiece to *The Jolly Pocket Postman*. There, a *mise en abyme* makes room for the reader: it ushers her in, makes her feel welcome, and suggests that there'll be more to this story than meets the eye.

FOR YOU

Figure 20 From *The Jolly Pocket Postman* by Janet and Allan Ahlberg

It can also be gratifying to spot a *mise en abyme* tucked away somewhere out of plain sight. Attentive readers of *The Pencil* will be pleased to see Allan ant clutching a tiny replica of the book as he makes his way across the tablecloth.

When *mises en abyme* take the form of stories within stories in literary texts, they become fictional microcosms which distill and replicate the narrative in miniature. The pattern tends to resonate beyond the final page, like a chain verse that forgoes closure and completion. The following extract from *The Phantom Tollbooth* demonstrates the form:

> 'Where could you keep anything so tiny?' Milo asked, trying very hard to imagine such a thing.
>
> The Mathemagician stopped what he was doing and explained simply, 'Why, in a box that's so small you can't see it – and that's kept in a drawer that's so small you can't see it, in a dresser that's so small you can't see it, in a house that's so small you can't see it, on a street that's so small you can't see it, in a city that's so small you can't see it, which is part of a country that's so small you can't see it, in a world that's so small you can't see it!'
>
> Then he sat down, fanned himself with a handkerchief and continued. 'Then of course, we keep the whole thing in another box that's so small you can't see it – and if you follow me, I'll show you where to find it.'[33]

The conceit is taken even further in *Charlie Cook's Favourite Book* by Julia Donaldson and Axel Scheffler. We encounter the first embedded image on the cover. Surrounded by a cast of storybook characters, Charlie is sitting in an armchair reading a copy of *Charlie Cook's Favourite Book*, every detail of its cover faithfully reproduced in miniature. There's a second *mise en abyme* in the frontispiece: Charlie with pirate, parrot and cat reading a book (we can't catch the title) with a smaller Charlie, pirate, parrot and cat reflected on the cover. But this is only the beginning. Charlie's *mise en abyme*-filled library in a book is made up of a series of nested stories representing a range of children's literary genres, seamlessly interwoven, in which the characters not only tell their own stories, but finally get to read their favorite book 'about a cosy armchair, and a boy called Charlie Cook.'

Mises en abyme can also serve thematic purposes. In *The Mouse and His Child*, Russell Hoban makes extensive use of embedding and mirror imagery to shed light on themes of connectedness and interdependence.

His focal point is an infinite procession of little black-and-white dogs on the label of a BONZO dog food can.

The BONZO label, which appears in various states of transformation throughout the text, is a fictional *mise en abyme par excellence*:

> BONZO Dog Food said the white letters on the orange label, and below the name was a picture of a little black-and-white spotted dog walking on his hind legs and wearing a chef's cap and apron. The dog carried a tray on which there was another can of BONZO Dog Food, on the label of which another little black-and-white spotted dog, exactly the same but much smaller, was walking on his hind legs and carrying a tray on which there was another can of BONZO Dog Food, on the label of which another little black-and-white spotted dog, exactly the same but much smaller, was walking on hind legs and carrying a tray on which there was another can of BONZO Dog Food, and so on until the dogs became too small for the eye to follow.[34]

It is the mouse child's fate to discover what lies beyond the last visible dog and this he tries to do, time and again. When he finally comes face to face with the answer reflected in the mirror of the BONZO can, he is able to draw on the cumulative perspectives projected by the many dogs who have accompanied him on his journey up to that point. These include Bonzo, the little black-and-white dog who sees the father and son set out on their quest; the multitude of BONZO-label dogs encountered along the way; and, presiding over all that transpires, Sirius the Dog Star, brightest star in the Great Dog constellation.

The narrative is framed by the mysterious figure of the tramp whose perspective enables the reader to enter the world of the clockwork mouse and his child for the first time. In the toy shop where their story begins, the mice live with a toy elephant and a little tin seal who spins a red and yellow ball on her nose. The mouse and his child share a single clockwork mechanism and they dance in a circle at the turn of a key. The tramp, watching the pair dance through the toy shop window, takes this perfect but unsustainable moment and re-enacts it in a dance of his own, transforming it and setting it free to shape the story. This accomplished, the tramp and his little black-and-white spotted dog disappear into the night.

The following day the mouse and his child are sold as Christmas gifts. For the next four years, every evening during the festive season, they dance and dance in endless circles leading nowhere. The fifth Christmas arrives and they are brought down from the attic as usual. On this particular night, however, the mouse child catches a glimpse of something new under the tree: a dolls' house, less imposing than the grand house in the toy store, but familiar enough to remind him of all that he has never known and all that he has lost. And though he knows no good will come of it, the mouse begins to cry. The family cat is so startled that she knocks over a vase which shatters the father and child. Thrown out with the rubbish, they end up in a tip on the outskirts of town, where they are found by the tramp and his little black-and-white dog.

Their reassembly, the first of a number of transformations which the mouse and his child undergo during the story, is only partially successful: various bits and pieces of clockwork have to be discarded during their restoration, with the result that they can only walk in a straight line. Now the mouse child walks backwards, eyes fixed on his father who leads the way.

Towards the end of their first day on the road, the mouse father and child are waylaid by Manny Rat, a villain who runs a windup slave racket out of the town dump. The relationship between mouse and child and Manny Rat is a curious mixture of the ironic, the metonymic, and the metaphoric. Manny is, after all, a flesh-and-blood caricature of the windup mice, their doppelgänger and their nemesis. Indeed, the role played by Manny Rat in pushing the mouse and his child towards victory is uncannily similar to that of their protector, the tramp, and the other benefactors they meet on their journey.

As Manny leads the father and child through the infernal landscape of the dump, Sirius, the Dog Star, surveys the dreadful scene below with a glittering light which reduces all it touches to insignificance. Manny averts his eyes, but the mouse child gazes back resolutely:

> if he was nothing, he thought, so also was this rat and all the dump.
> His father's hands were firm upon his, and he resolved to see what
> next the great world offered.[35]

What Manny's domain offers is a ghastly parody of the toy shop, where headless dolls dance the hula by candlelight and battered windup scavengers (their days as tumbling clowns and dancing bears long over) wait to see who will be the next to end up in the spare-parts bin (complete with its BONZO label). As the mouse father looks on helplessly, an ailing clockwork donkey is swiftly despatched and cast into the BONZO can by one of Manny's henchmen. This is enough for the father, who decides they must escape any way they can.

And so their dangerous journey begins. After many trials, tests and adventures the mouse and his child find themselves stuck in the mud at the bottom of a pond. This is the preserve of Serpentina, playwright (the mice had a small role in his experimental project 'The Last Visible Dog') and deep turtle-thinker. He proposes a seemingly impossible challenge. The child must discover what lies beyond the last visible dog still visible on the disintegrating label of a submerged BONZO can.

The months go by and the child continues to stare at the label. As he does so, negotiating the playframes enclosing each little dog's individual playworld, he is replicating the role of the reader in this intricately patterned, playful text. To make sense of the story, the reader has to read *through*, *under* and *around* the layered narrative, making the required connections in exactly the same way the mouse child does when he navigates the nested/superimposed playworlds which unfold before his gaze.

Spring turns into summer as snails and algae make themselves at home in what's left of the mouse child's fur. A dragonfly helps him focus on the task, but no matter how hard they concentrate, the mouse child always loses his place before he reaches the smallest dog still recognisable as a dog on the BONZO can. The days drag on while the mouse father watches helplessly, 'infinity at his back.'

Then, one still morning, the mouse child takes the final leap. Beyond the last visible dog he sees tiny dots of color and between them blank white space, the emptiness of nothing at all, flowing into the smallest dog and out through the largest in an everlasting dance. When the last vestiges of the BONZO label drift away and the mouse child recognizes his own image in the mirror of the BONZO can, everything falls into focus: there is nothing beyond the last visible dog but the child and his father, the gathering of friends and enemies who have brought them this far and, in the background, the tramp who keeps watch.

Encouraged by this discovery, the tattered tin mice continue on their way. Wound to dance in a circle out in the world, the mice eventually return to the place where their journey began – back to the dump and, in the middle of the dump, to the dolls' house which has ended up in the rubbish. It is there that they make their home with the toys who have joined them along the way.

One evening, an abject Manny Rat appears at their doorstep, looking for shelter and work. The family is sceptical but eventually agrees. Manny comes up with a plan for illuminating the dolls' house and offers to help the mouse and his child with the problem of self-winding.

> 'Ungoing into going and back again,' muttered Manny Rat, and tried
> to sense how energy released by one spring could be made to wind
> another spring.[36]

Seeing the connections, he rearranges rods and gears and reassembles the motors. Returning to consciousness, the mouse and his child find that they can walk unaided.

Meanwhile, Manny's other project is nearing completion. That night, the dolls' house will be flooded with light. As the final preparations fall into place, the elephant notices a tangle of wires and powder scattered on the floor. She tidies up the mess, reversing the direction of the charge (Manny had planned to blow them all up) and electrifying the hapless rat. He recovers, though, and takes his place in the family as Uncle Manny (after all, 'everyone can't be nice'[37]). The dolls' house opens its doors as The Last Visible Dog ('shelter and good cheer for the weary traveller') and the mouse and his child find, when their self-winding mechanisms finally run down, that they are content to leave the winding to their friends.

That Christmas eve, at the first stroke of midnight, two travellers tumble out of the freight train as it makes its way around the dump. With the little black-and-white dog by his side, the tramp looks through the brightly lit window of The Last Visible Dog

> and he smiled and spoke to the mouse and his child for the second
> time.
> 'Be happy,' said the tramp.[38]

The structure of *The Mouse and His Child* is playfully recursive, unfolding in a series of spiral movements which mirrors the progress of the clockwork mice who are impelled, paradoxically, to go out into the world and to dance in a circle at the same time. The visible dog *mise en abyme* lies at the center of this ever-diminishing movement, a playful device which represents the process of coming into being and the theme of coming into being in connection with others. This theme is underscored by the use of dialogical forms such as riddles and prophecies, the application of nonsense strategies which suggest unexpected connections between things, and the foregrounding of figures – puns in particular – which reveal multiple meanings in a single word or proposition. With these features in mind, it is time to turn our attention to the subject of wordplay and nonsense in other playful texts for young readers.

Language play, visual games and nonsense

Metafictive texts for children frequently play with words and images in ways which highlight textuality and the construction of meaning. Texts may incorporate visual puzzles and optical illusions, foreground patterns of rhythm and rhyme, and have fun with linguistic playforms such as anagrams, rebuses, riddles and puns. They may indulge in verbal and visual nonsense, and explore the world-making functions of metaphor and other figurative forms of expression. Let's start where many beginners start: with Dr. Seuss and his Cat in the Hat.

The Cat in the Hat has been beguiling readers for over 50 years. Written (in perfect anapaestic tetrameter) specifically for children just beginning to read on their own, this exciting and intensely energetic text zips along at an exhilarating pace. Its sequel, *The Cat in the Hat Comes Back*, displays the same 'wild restraint'[39] (breathless but tightly controlled metrical forms, meticulous rhymes and riotous action) but introduces more distinctly metafictive elements to heighten the reading experience.

The Cat in the Hat Comes Back explores the connections to be made between good sense (beware of cats in stovepipe hats, especially when they've tricked you before), common sense (pink cat rings are almost impossible to banish from bathtubs – never use a white dress for this purpose), and nonsense (in an emergency you can call on Little Cats A–X, and if all else fails ask Little Cat Z to unleash 'Voom': it's hidden under his hat). Seussian rhymes highlight the array of mystifying propositions children have to negotiate to make sense of the world. This is a never-ending process, of course, and one which is illuminated by the creative power of the imagination – another capacity celebrated by Seuss.

Dr. Seuss's nonsensical verses 'lodge in his readers' heads and, like all great poetry, enlarge their sense of what language – their language – can do.'[40] Like his literary predecessors Edward Lear and Mervyn Peake, Seuss was drawn to the metalinguistic resources of the alphabet. He gave prominent roles to alphabetical characters in *The Cat in the Hat Comes Back* and produced a nonsense alphabet: *Dr. Seuss's ABC*. His most audacious experiment, however, was *On Beyond Zebra*, first published in 1955.

In *On Beyond Zebra*, the narrator creates a new alphabet which goes where no other alphabet has gone, on beyond Z to reveal letters such as YUZZ (as in Yuzz-a-ma-Tuzz), WUM (for Wumbus), UM (for Umbus), FUDDLE (Miss Fuddle-dee-Duddle), GLIKK (for Glikker), SNEE (for Sneedle), QUAN (Quandry), and a yet to be translated final character comprising all the letters A-Z endlessly entangled. While readers may be quick to discern the underlying pattern here (each sign is a monogram made up of at least two conventional English letters), the letters, accompanied by the fantastic animals after which they are named, are considerably more than the sum of their parts. These hybrid characters challenge the limits of things in classic nonsensical fashion, playing with closed systems and categorization, the literal and the imaginary, to produce an open-ended text which celebrates creativity and hypothetical thinking. This is an alphabet which urges young readers to pay attention to detail, ask questions, and look beneath the surface of things – 'to go beyond Z and start poking around!'

Other alphabet books focus on the sounds of language, its timbre, cadence, rhythm and rhymes. Bill Martin Jr. and John Archambault employ scat syllables and jazz inflections to fine effect in their celebrated alphabet song, *Chicka Chicka Boom Boom*. When lower case 'a' dares its friends 'b' and 'c' to 'meet at the top of the coconut tree' it doesn't stop to think what will happen when the other letters of the alphabet scramble to join them. Capitals come running as the small letters tumble to the ground, characters akimbo, 'looped,' 'stooped,' and 'twisted, alley-oop.'

In her alphabet puzzle, *Eye Spy*, Linda Bourke explores the meaning-making potential of two specific groups of words that rhyme: homonyms and homophones. She also inserts an additional visual clue in the final frame of each series so that meanings ripple through the text, creating subtle semiotic patterns as they disperse. So we have for the letter 'C', three images of water birds (a Sarus-, a Sandhill- and a Red-Crowned Crane) and one of a machine, with a boom and a hook, hoisting a giant die. Turning the page to 'D', we find three colored dice and a pair of hands dipping a scrap of cloth into a tub of 'New Look' fabric dye. The winking-eye logo on the box invites us to turn over to the letter 'E', and so on. 'V' for 'vane/vain' is a triumph.

Taking an entirely different approach, *The Disappearing Alphabet* by Richard Wilbur and David Diaz considers what the world would be like if the alphabet began to fade away. Vanishing letters create real-world dilemmas: cows are reduced to munching 'hy;' birds have to cope with wigs instead of wings; and, without the letter 'y', there's no way of saying 'yes' or even 'maybe.' Helpfully, the text also highlights the fact that letters can have many diverse functions. Treasure maps are rendered useless without 'x' to mark the spot, and whole symphonies suffer when they are deprived of 'C' major. Finally, putting everything in perspective, we're reminded that losing the Roman numeral 'M' would mean losing a thousand years.

Learning to read involves coming to terms with the semantic complexities of English. Words may sound the same but have entirely different meanings, as the examples in *Eye Spy* reveal. Meanings may be slightly different, or slightly different in different contexts. While nouns rarely have antonyms (what would be the opposite of 'fish'?), synonyms are another matter. Synonyms proliferate in their own right ('boat'/'ship'/'yacht') or as members of groups or classes ('furniture': 'table, 'chair', 'desk' and 'sofa'). And yet every word carries its own connotation. Is 'cloth' really synonymous with 'fabric'? This is a fertile area for language play, and playful texts have taken it up.

In *The Phantom Tollbooth*, King Azaz the Unabridged, monarch of Dictionopolis, sends five advisers to greet Milo and his watchdog, Tock.

'We offer you the hospitality of our kingdom,'

'Country,'
'Nation,'
'State,'
'Commonwealth,'
'Realm,'
'Empire,'
'Palatinate,'
'Principality.'
'Do all those words mean the same thing?' gasped Milo.
'Of course.'
'Certainly.'
'Precisely.'
'Exactly.'
'Yes,' they replied in order.
'Well then,' said Milo, not understanding why each one said the same thing in a slightly different way, 'wouldn't it be simpler to use just one? It would certainly make more sense.'
'Nonsense.'
'Ridiculous.'
'Fantastic.'
'Absurd.'[41]

Scieszka and Smith's *Baloney (Henry P.)*, represents a variation on the same theme. The premise is as follows. Henry P. Baloney is late for school and is facing lifelong detention unless he has a very good excuse. Fortunately, he does. As Henry tells his teacher, he was about to leave home when he realized he'd misplaced his *zimulis*. He found it hidden away on his desk, but someone had put his desk in a *torakku*. The *torakku* drove him to *szkola*, but wouldn't stop, so he jumped out, landing smack in the middle of a *razzo* launch pad. And so on … Henry lands on the planet Astrosus. He charms the Astrosians with his clever *piksas* and *giadrams* (thank heavens for his *zimulis*), finally escapes and goes more or less straight to *szkola*.

This nimble text recreates, with its parade of multilingual synonyms and anagrams, the experience, familiar to developing readers, of learning to read when every second word looks like it comes from outer space. It demonstrates clearly how readers have to use contextual clues within the fictional world of the text to interpret words they do not understand. While the illustrations assist in this process, most of the images are presented in a stylized manner which defies straightforward interpretation. Further, by assuming the form of a linguistic puzzle, the text challenges readers to play the meaning-making game for its own sake and then prompts them to go back a second time (equipped with solutions supplied in a decoder at the back of the book) and read the story in a different light.

In his clever picturebook, *Mr Wuffles!*, David Wiesner turns a linguistic puzzle into a masterclass in cryptography. Comprising no less than three invented languages and a few words of English, the narrative offers a series of metalinguistic lessons for intrepid readers. The story of alien visitors who forge a partnership with household insects to outwit Mr Wuffles the cat is told from multiple points of view. As will become clear in this chapter, the polyphonic quality of the text is characteristic of playful picturebooks and novels; here it is distinctly metalinguistic in focus, highlighting the structure of language and patterns of word formation.

The invented languages share certain conventions which help to ease readers into the puzzle of the text. Dialogue is indicated by word balloons: rectangular for the aliens, smooth and rounded for the insects, oval for human speech and jagged for Mr Wuffles. Punctuation marks are also used to modify comments and underscore intense emotion.

Decoding Cat is quite straightforward. 'MROWW!' Mr Wuffles cries as the aliens' spacecraft escapes his grasp. Insect is more opaque: little more than clusters of tiny claw marks, with or without paragraphs, whose meanings can only really be gleaned from context. The insects are artists, not authors, and their history is represented in Lascaux-like murals which tell of their battles with previous generations of cats.

The aliens' written language is of another order altogether. It is composed of a set of 30 geometric symbols – circles and quartered circles, triangles, rectangles, ellipses and spirals – displayed as single units or as composite entities resembling fractions, each with its own 'numerator' and 'denominator'. The controlled repetition of forms produces a language with a discernible structure.[42] It has basic lexical units (a triangle, say, or an unadorned circle) which can be inflected in various ways. Let's assume the root word (an equilateral triangle) represents a state of excitement or wonder. Manipulating the root, inserting an isosceles triangle or a right-angled scalene, allows for greater nuance and precision. The circle, on the other hand, seems to suggest movement. It can be slowed down (as a semicircle, a plump oval or a tottering ellipse) or spun into a spinning wheel turning on its axis. The possibilities multiply as symbols are sliced and sectioned, twisted and turned upside down. This, coupled with the splitting, embedding and superimposition of symbols, creates a rich, intricate language capable of conveying complex thoughts and emotions. As mentioned, modifiers (stylized exclamation points and question marks) are used to deepen the interpersonal dimension of the discourse, as are gestures, facial expressions and eye movements. For readers, the interpretative possibilities are legion.

It seems reasonable to expect invented languages to contain neologisms, and to insist on creating new words for the sheer joy of it. Andrew Clements examines this idea in *Frindle*, an account of the war of words which develops when a student coins a new word for 'pen' ('frindle') and the name catches on.

Words can, of course, simply become tired and run out of meaning through overuse. Playful texts may exploit this phenomenon, employing clichés, headlines and the language of advertising to explore the limits of meaningful language. In the following scene from *The Mouse and His Child*, toys take tea in their dolls' house:

> It was the elephant's constant delight to watch that tea party
> through the window, and as the hostess she took great pride in the
> quality of her hospitality. 'Have another cup of tea,' she said to one
> of the ladies. 'Try a little pastry.'
>
> 'HIGH-SOCIETY SCANDAL, changing to cloudy, with a possibility of
> BARGAINS GALORE!' replied the lady. Her papier-mâché head made
> of paste and newsprint, she always spoke in scraps of news and
> advertising, in whatever order they came to mind.
> 'Bucket seats,' remarked the gentleman next to her. 'Power steering
> optional. GOVERNMENT FALLS.'[43]

Clichés can also be appropriated and given new life in fresh and surprising images.

> 'Be very quiet,' advised the duke, 'for it goes without saying.'
> And, sure enough, as soon as they were all quite still, it began to move
> quickly through the streets, and in a very short time they arrived at
> the royal palace.[44]

Freshly-minted words, phrases and images can depict different worlds
of meaning bumping into one another or completely converging. Using the
metacommunicative cues characteristic of make-believe play, playful texts
often foreground figurative language and illustrations (especially verbal/
visual puns, similes and metaphors) to highlight the resemblances between
things while simultaneously making room for different perspectives. These
are precisely the effects achieved when Cinderella's page-boy, Roger, pronounces 'I was a rat' (Philip Pullman, *I Was a Rat!... or The Scarlet* Slippers);
a drama school for crows calls itself the 'Caws of Art' (*The Mouse and His
Child*); or Rabbit's local restaurant, 'The Burrowed Wok,' offers free Lawn
Crackers and Morning Dew (Emily Gravett, *Wolves*).

There are numerous examples of sustained tropic play to be found in
wordless texts, multimodal fictions and metafictive novels. I will focus on
three very different texts to demonstrate what is possible.

In *My Heart Is Like a Zoo*, Michael Hill takes a simple simile, decon-
structs it to reveal its many moods and dimensions ('My heart is like a
zoo – ... silly as a seal ... angry as a bear, bothered as a bull with a hornet
in its hair ...'),[45] and represents this menagerie of feelings entirely in heart
shapes – more than three hundred in all. The proliferation of shapes creates
an intricate visual pattern which is reflected, in the written text, by the use
of verbal patterning in the form of alliteration, consonance and rhyme. The
digital images are bright and engaging, employing a range of shades across
the color spectrum. The lion's face on the front cover is particularly striking
– he's such an expansive figure his mane spills over the edges of the page.[46]
On the back cover we are given, in a magnanimous self-reflexive gesture,
an insight into the way this image was composed, layer by layer, beginning
with a single red heart for the lion's mane, an inverted orange heart (with
two black dots) for his face, then a small heart-shaped nose and a yellow
heart-shaped chin set slightly off-center, with a final snip here and there to
give the mane some shagginess.

In *Anno's Peekaboo*, hand puppets function as dramatic stage characters, helping young readers develop a concept of sustained narrative

through role play. Role switching is accompanied throughout the text by unexpected shifts in orientation and point of view. In practice, these shifts in perspective would be accompanied by a real-world, out-of-frame dialogue (*Anno's Peekaboo* is a wordless text) as the adult reader clarifies the events that are unfolding on the page. As mentioned in Chapter 2, the game proceeds in the typical manner, with the implicit message 'this is play' (two hands obscuring the puppet), and the revelation – 'peekaboo!'

Figure 21 From *Anno's Peekaboo* by Mitsumasa Anno

But then another set of playrules is imposed on the peekaboo scheme, altering it completely.

Figure 22 From *Anno's Peekaboo* by Mitsumasa Anno

For all of their surprises, the initial play sequences allow for a certain degree of parallelism and repetition as the young reader becomes accustomed to the rules of the game (peekaboo with a twist), and becomes more practiced in their execution. The use of visual close-ups and eye-to-eye contact allows a dialogical relationship to develop between reader and text. This sense of connectedness is reinforced by the fact that each subsequent image retains something of the shape, color and texture of the one preceding it, creating a sense of metonymy and inter-relationship as the transformations proceed.

This pattern is disrupted, however, by an abrupt turn in the narrative as the tiger transforms into a quick succession of unexpected puppet figures: mother, child, father, pig (!), fox, teddy-bear, clown and Santa Claus. This dazzling series of metamorphoses – in which visual pun and metaphor, metonymy and synecdoche, irony and paradox jostle for attention – mirrors and recontextualizes the opening frames of the text, so that readers, armed with what they've learned about the playful nature of the book, can pick up the joke and run with it.

The third text is Lauren Child's picturebook, *I Will Not Ever Never Eat a Tomato*. Charlie has trouble coaxing his little sister Lola to eat her dinner until he devises a very smart plan. Lola can't stand carrots or peas or potatoes but succumbs when they're transformed into 'orange twiglets' from Jupiter, prized Greenlandic 'green drops', and delectable 'cloud fluff' all the way from Mount Fuji. And just when that seems to be the end of the matter, Lola turns the tables on Charlie in a shrewd move of her own:

> And I can't believe my eyes because guess what she is pointing at,
> the *tomatoes*.
> And I say, 'Are you sure? Really? One of these?'
> And she says, 'Yes, of course, *moonsquirters* are my favourites.
> You didn't think they were tomatoes, did you, Charlie?'[47]

Lauren Child's illustrations augment the story very well. The artwork – a digital collage of watercolors, photomontage and magazine cuttings – brings Charlie's metaphors to life with great flair. Odd textures, juxtaposed 2D and 3D images, unusual page layout, retro styling and erratic fonts combine to transform the domestic setting into a playworld which the children share.

We have seen some of the ways in which figurative forms of expression – metaphors and their kin – can animate a text, creating a joyful experience for the youngest of readers. There is, however, another dimension of semiotic playfulness to which we need to return: literary nonsense.

Metaphors have the ability to change reality, creating alternative ways of looking at the world and everything in it. The aims of nonsense are quite different. Nonsense worlds are not metaphoric: they are meant to be taken literally. Nonsense insists on taking a ridiculous proposition and following it, scrupulously, to its conclusion. I have chosen a range of nonsense texts which exemplify this process.

Let's start with some generic nonsense. *The Worm Book* by Janet and Allan Ahlberg is a nonsensical handbook: a complete guide to worm care and the history of *wormus wormus*. Nonsense delights in systems of classification and *The Worm Book* captures its obsessions precisely. There are faux scientific names, distribution tables and definitions.

> All good worms have a beginning, a middle and an end.
> Worms with two beginnings, a middle and no end are apt to injure themselves.
> Worms with two ends, a middle and no beginning get bored.[48]

The handbook also contains worm hunting tips and a training regime; a list of common ailments and their treatment; and a survey of specialized skills (mountain rescue worms, worms in wartime, the Bertram Worm Circus, clockwork worms and other oddities). The comparative study of worms is instructive:

> In some parts of the world the worm is treated as a sacred animal. Statues and fountains are put up in his honour.
>
> In other parts of the world the worm is treated as a sausage. Plates of worms are served with eggs, and the wormburger is a popular snack.[49]

Nonsense classification can go much further than this, though, plundering the specialist discourses of science, mathematics and philosophy for its own ends. *The Mouse and His Child* illustrates this tendency in a remarkable way.

In their quest to become self-winding, the clockwork mouse and his child come across Muskrat, experimental scientist and proponent of the groundbreaking Much-in-Little Theorem. (There are many variations, but the formula *Why* × *How* = *What* sums it up.) Eager for new students, Muskrat treats the mouse and his child to an intensive course in applied much-in-little thought.

The lessons are intriguing at first. They take place in Muskrat's den, which is littered with the debris of previous experiments. The products of Muskrat's labors constitute a bizarre inventory of who knows what.

An oilcan and a ball of string lay among the mussel shells and the forgotten nibbled ends of roots and stalks beside a small terrestrial pencil-sharpener globe; a BONZO Dog Food can stood filled with salvage from the bottom of the pond ... Near it sprawled improvisations of discolored pipe cleaners, tobacco tins, old fishing-licence badges, draggled wet- and dry-fly feathers, coils of catgut, jointed lures that bristled with hooks and staring eyes – all the neglected apparatus of past experiments in applied thought. Against the wall leaned a bit of broken slate with X's, Y's and Z's scrawled on it. The air was warm, the odour studious and strong.[50]

The mouse and his child are diligent students but Muskrat's new theoretical project – to prove that $XT = T^F$ (*Axe times Tree equals Treefall*) – almost proves fatal, and the mice are fortunate to escape with their lives.

Nonsense also challenges the boundaries of discourse. As we saw in *The Worm Book*, things don't really make sense unless they have a beginning and an end. Chain verses and deeply repetitive structures are well suited to this kind of nonsense, as demonstrated by Scieszka and Adel's metafictive version of 'The house that Jack built.'

This is the Book that Jack wrote.
This is the Picture
That lay in the Book that Jack wrote.
...
This is the Book that Jack wrote,
That squashed the Man in the tattered coat,
That stomped the Bug, that frayed the rug,
That tripped the Hatter in the hall,
That knocked the Egg falling off the wall,
That startled the Pieman at the fair,
That flung the Pie flying through the air,
That beaned the Baby humming the tune,
That tossed the Cow sailing over the moon,
That spooked the Dog,
That chased the Rat,
That fell in the Picture ...
That lay in the Book that Jack Wrote.[51]

Figure 23 From *The Book that Jack Wrote* by Jon Scieszka and Daniel Adel

Like other forms of make-believe play, nonsense is paradoxical in nature. It is precise and meticulous, and yet it revels in excess and ambiguity. Works of visual nonsense overflow with intricate optical illusions and indeterminate signs, visual puns and hybrid creatures.

Consider the cover of David Legge's *Bamboozled*. A little girl sits on a sofa in her grandad's living room. His portrait (face only, simply framed) hangs on the wall behind her. But something is very wrong with this picture. The broad shouldered sofa is neatly dressed in brown serge, offset by a blue business shirt and red tie (with eyes). Its arms are comfortably padded – but those arms are trimmed with crisp blue cuffs and a realistic pair of grandfatherly hands! This startling image is the first in a gallery of illusions and trompe l'oeil effects which create strange tricks of perspective, disorienting readers who make their way through the text without the benefit of context or other sense-making supports. *Bamboozled* takes a lot of unraveling, but the text is irresistible.

While it is always assured in execution, visual nonsense can assume many different moods. In the enigmatic picturebook lullaby, *Goodnight Moon* (by Margaret Wise Brown and Clement Hurd), the narrator offers a whispered goodnight wish to a plain white page. 'Goodnight nobody,' she says.

I will complete this survey of language play and visual nonsense with Shaun Tan's picturebook, *The Lost Thing*, a text which draws together many of the themes and techniques discussed in this section. *The Lost Thing* encourages readers to be mindful and pay attention to superfluous things which have no obvious place in society. To argue its case, the narrative takes the form of a nonsense compendium, with many of the genre's characteristics – the matter-of-fact tone and obsession with list-making and classification; the fascination with the minutiae of science and industry; and the propensity for semiotic overload – prominently displayed.

Set in a dark, 'retro-future' suburb,[52] *The Lost Thing* is packed with people engaging in all kinds of activities, but the monotone world it portrays is strangely static and lifeless, almost paralysed. There is simply too much concrete (towering embankments of concrete, pillars and roadways and funnels and pipes), and too much *meaning*: too many inscrutable signs (charts, tables, diagrams, formulae and equations), pointless instructions, impossible directions and preposterous machines, cogs, cables and wires.

The lost thing who wanders into the story is clearly an anomaly in this overly meaningful world. It is a large, red, watery creature who is quite difficult to describe, looking a little like a teapot, a crab and an industrial boiler. Befriended by the narrator, it eventually finds a home with a raggle-taggle group of other lost things who simply don't belong anywhere else.

Like the strange creature who gives the story its name, *The Lost Thing* is a fascinating hybrid. The text is a collage of handwritten captions pasted over old physics and engineering textbooks. Carefully arranged in the manner of a stamp collection or photograph album, the pages are interspersed with extraordinary images. As John Stephens has observed, Shaun Tan's artwork blends elements of surrealism, comic book art and steampunk (a baroque fantasy genre which combines beautifully crafted Victorian steam-engines and scientific devices with modern technology) with references to classic Australian paintings such as John Brack's *Collins St., 5p.m.* and Jeffrey Smart's *Cahill Expressway*.[53] The artwork creates an overwhelming sense of alienation, relieved only by the scenes in which the lost thing – a shambolic, whimsical figure – glows with its own inner light.

There is a certain whimsy, too, in the word games and metafictive gestures which are scattered throughout the text. The government agencies are inspired:

- **The Department of Odds and Ends** – motto: *sweepus underum carpetae* (emblem: a flying pig).
- **The Department of Economics** – *consumer ergo sum* (a blind piggy bank).

- **The Department of Pipes and Tubes** – *plumbiferus ductus* (a transparent pig with gizmos and gaskets).
- **The Department of Information** – *ignorare regulatum* (a puzzled pig).
- **The Department of Censorship** – *illūmināre prohibitus* (a blindfolded pig).

And, on the back cover, there's a final endorsement by Government Inspector 920756/07, confirming that the volume is safe for public consumption: 'No perceptible threat to the order of day to day existence.'

Intertextuality and polyphony

Playful texts are generous texts, capable of accommodating multiple narrative voices, view points and allusions. While *all* of the books discussed so far have intertextual elements, some works are more dialogical than others. We have seen how metafiction likes to draw on the intertext of children's culture – its nursery rhymes, folk tales, fairy stories, cartoons and comics – to explore the codes and conventions of storytelling, but we have not considered the subject of intertextuality in its own right. I'd like to conclude this survey of textual playfulness with a selection of texts which flaunt their intertextuality in bold and imaginative ways.

We'll begin with a series which sets the standard for playful intertextuality: *The Jolly Postman* books. Immersed in the culture of children's stories,[54] these joyful texts give substance to the notion of intertext by including miniature books, pull-out board games, circulars, maps and letters for the reader to interpret. This has proved to be a winning device, and it has since been copied many times.

In *The Jolly Pocket Postman*, the Postman, dazed by a nasty knock on the head by a giant rattle, trips down a rabbit hole, makes the mistake of having tea with Alice, and finds that he has shrunk to pocket size. Beset by dangers, he manages to climb *through* a postage stamp (there's lots of frame breaking in this text too) and into the envelope which is fixed to the facing page. Inside there's a tiny toy box which opens up to reveal a regiment of tin soldiers, one Postman, one Postman's dog, and a neatly folded story.

The embedded story hurtles along, eventually ending up in the Duchess's kitchen.

> But – no time for rhyme, no time for coincidences – the Postman, still
> in peril, about to be cooked for tea – fish and Postman Pie, O my! –
> hears giant voices … Oh dear we're running out of space – can you read
> this at the back? Anyway, the Postman sees his chance – the baby and the
> cook are sneezing – and tiptoes from the pie dish. 'We're getting out of here!'
> he tells the dog. And they do.[55]

Sliding out of the envelope, the Postman bounces back into the narrative proper, where he joins Dorothy and her companions (the enclosed map skirts Old McDonald's Farm, passes through the Looking-Glass, and avoids Mr McGregor's garden), catches up with Alice again, and is knocked over by the Gingerbread Boy on his bicycle. Recovering in Cock Robin Memorial Hospital, the Postman (now restored to his former size) receives a card from Dorothy and Alice ('Greetings from Emerald City'):

> Here we are! Made it! Alice right size now. **Dorothy magicked me
> with her ruby slippers.** – Tin man has a heart and so on. – **The
> Hatter a better hat – Gingerbread boy an improved flavour.** Off to
> Kansas soon. – **The Wizard's balloon.** – Alice is coming to stay. **Yes!
> Yippee!** Bye bye for now, **Alice**, Dorothy and Toto. P.S. On the way
> we met a nice boy – Peter Pan – Alice loves him – **No Dorothy does!
> P.P.S. Did we dream you** – or did you dream us?[56]

In a final twist, the postcard is slipped into the sleeve of a little booklet that presents an alternative version of the day's events. This story – *If the Tyre Had Not Been Flat* – would, the authors suggest, probably appeal to readers who enjoyed other titles in the series such as *If the Bears Had Phoned the Police* and *If the Cupboard Had Been Full*.

The dialogue between text and intertext in *The Jolly Postman* books is quite open and explicit: readers are likely to recognize the original settings, characters and plots, and enjoy the ways in which these elements have been manipulated. In other metafictive texts, the identification of intertextual references becomes a challenge in itself. In Philip Pullman's *I Was a Rat! … or The Scarlet Slippers*, the reader is given clues to the hero's identity but no satisfactory explanation until the end.

The story goes like this. One cold, moonlit night, Bob the shoemaker opens his door to a small boy in a tattered page boy's uniform. 'Bless my soul,' said Bob. 'Who are you?' 'I was a rat,' said the little boy. Bob and Joan, his wife, take the boy in. They call him Roger and set about finding his family.

Roger is appreciative and eager to please but he has some unusual habits which are difficult to break. The interview at City Hall, for example, ends badly when Roger consumes the office stationery.

News of the boy who believes he's a rat eventually reaches the Palace, and the Philosopher Royal conducts his own philosophical investigations. Roger is well informed about the workings of the royal household, but the consultation is terminated after an incident with the philosopher's cat. Then everything unravels. Roger is kidnapped, exhibited as an abominable *Rat-Boy!!*, and pressed into service for a gang of thieves. *The Daily Scourge* newspaper wages a vicious campaign against him, and calls for his life. Then, at the last moment, Princess Aurelia (formerly Mary Jane, kitchen maid) intervenes on Roger's behalf. He discards his former life, happy to become an apprentice shoemaker.

Philip Pullman blends Victorian melodrama and contemporary social commentary in his version of the Cinderella story. Shifts in tone are handled with grace and agility, producing a text which is gleeful one moment and grave the next. The satirical elements of the story are particularly incisive, with *The Daily Scourge* serving as a powerful symbol of hypocrisy and opportunism.

As mentioned in my discussion of dialogical reading, playful texts tend to emphasize the polyphonic qualities of narrative fiction, allowing many voices to speak through the text. In Anthony Browne's picturebook, *Voices in the Park*, the interplay of narrative voices produces a profoundly dialogical text.

The author revisits a picturebook which he wrote 20 years earlier (*A Walk in the Park*) and translates it as a complex, multilayered metafiction. The key elements of the plot remain the same. Mr Smith, his daughter, Smudge and their dog, Albert go for a walk in the park. So do Mrs Smythe, her son, Charles and their dog, Victoria. The Smiths and the Smythes inhabit vastly different socio-economic worlds and the parents ignore each other. Their dogs play together, however, and the children become friends.

Where the earlier text presented a single world and a single, effaced narrator, *Voices in the Park* offers a plurality of worlds – four distinct versions of the original story, each one complete in itself yet dependent on the others to make a meaningful narrative. (See Chapter 6 – 'Responding to *Voices in the Park*' – for an insight into the ways young readers negotiate the story's unusual structure.)

As the story moves from one voice to another, the landscape of the park changes to reflect the perspective of the narrator: clipped autumn foliage for Charles' mother, every leaf and tendril firmly in its place, while trees burst into flame just beyond her line of vision; a harsh winter skyline for Mr Smith, illuminated momentarily by Smudge's irrepressible presence; a bleak and forbidding backdrop for Charles, playfully transformed into the promise of spring; and, for Smudge, bright, saturated summer colors that leap off the page.

Voices in the Park celebrates the power of perspective taking and hypothetical thinking. Anthony Browne wants children 'to see the world through other people's eyes – to imagine what it's like to be somebody else.'[57] Such an intrinsically playful vision lends itself to textual playfulness, and much of the playfulness in *Voices* entails intertextual play. The zoomorphic characters (all, apart from the dogs, have gorilla heads and human bodies) stand in intertextual relationship to the protagonists of Browne's *Gorilla* and the *Willy* series; while Victoria and Albert create their own intertextual partnership, with a tiny queen (see opening 2) and a coronet-tipped lamp post (opening 12) completing the picture.

This type of intertextual maneuver is repeated throughout the book, creating a tapestry of associations and allusions. The textual fabric is actually made up of intratextual motifs (the many shape-shifting shadows, flaming trees and surrealist lamp posts which recur throughout the book) and intertextual references to well-known paintings (*Mona Lisa*, *The Scream*, and *The Laughing Cavalier*), children's literature (*Mary Poppins*, 'The Three Bears' and at least one fairy tale castle), and popular culture (*The Magic Roundabout*, *Dr Who*, and King Kong in various guises).

In *The Shaggy Gully Times*, Jackie French and Bruce Whatley celebrate one of the most intertextual of all print media, the local newspaper. *The Shaggy Gully Times* – 'we bring you the gnus as it happens' – is crammed with non sequiturs, puns, spoonerisms, idiosyncratic spelling, inappropriate captions, rude editorial comments, and scandalmongering. Playfulness permeates every aspect of the paper, from the masthead and the classifieds to the cryptic crossword.

The Shaggy Gully Times is an entertaining introduction to journalism and the vagaries of the newspaper business, with a harassed editor, Mothball Wombat, struggling to correct typesetting errors (at one point the letters 'u', 'r' 'p' and 'b' are stolen from the printers) and clarify misunderstandings (such as that posed by the zebra seen crossing the zebra crossing outside Shaggy Gully Central School). In true community newspaper spirit, *The Times* has taken up the cause of the unhappy animals at Mr Nasty's Zoo and many of the articles contain getaway tips for escapees.

Radical polyphony can be found in the most unlikely places. In Emily Gravett's comic story, *The Rabbit Problem*, a single intertext runs amok, proliferating at such a rate that it consumes the narrative, filling every inch of story space.

The Rabbit Problem re-enacts a mathematical conundrum posed by Fibonacci in the thirteenth century: If a pair of rabbits are put into a field, how many pairs will there be: (a) at the end of each month? and (b) after one year? Problem stated, the text turns into a calendar and proceeds to calculate the answer a month at a time, enlisting a host of Fibonacci spin-offs in the process.

January.   Lonely Rabbit sits in Fibonacci's Field and invites a friend to join her.
Population: 1

February.   Chalk Rabbit and Lonely Rabbit snuggle up in Fibonacci's Field. Other ways to keep warm are detailed in knitting patterns supplied by *Fibonacci Wools*.
Population: 1 pair

March.   They're parents. The babies' first weeks are recorded in an album published by Fibonacci Press.
Population: 2 pairs.

April.   Batten down the hatches: it's pouring. Need to book swimming lessons for the new arrivals.
Population: 3 pairs

May.   The Ministry of Carrots has issued ration coupons for the growing family in Fibonacci's Field.
Population: 5 pairs

June.   *Fibonacci Lettuce and Carrot Seeds* arrive just in time for planting. Situation critical.
Population: 8 pairs

July   Watching carrots grow. Boredom and bad tempers. Special issue of *The Fibber* produced: 'Birth rates rise!' (Attentive readers will also find a very important clue to Fibonacci's conundrum in this edition of the paper.)
Population: 13 pairs

August   Have any readers cracked the code?[58]

September   Yes, population: 34 pairs

And the months go by until ...

December   Population: 233 pairs

The Rabbit Problem fills all dimensions of story space with beautifully designed fold-outs and inserts (thank you *Jolly Postman*). These miniatures (recipe books, knitting patterns and seed packets) take the Fibonacci intertext into unexpected territory – slowly leading the reader deeper and deeper into the increasingly chaotic world of the burrow. Nothing, however, can prepare for the explosive conclusion, when the rabbits literally burst out of the text.

I will close this chapter with another story which spends much of its time underground: Terry Pratchett's deeply intertextual novel for older readers, *The Amazing Maurice and His Educated Rodents.*

The Amazing Maurice is a formal exercise in extreme perspective taking. The main story, a comic recreation of *The Pied Piper of Hamelin*, takes place in a backwater town in the outer reaches of Discworld, a flat disc of a world carried on the backs of four elephants supported by a giant turtle floating through space (but that's another story). It transpires that Maurice, a wisecracking Puss in Boots figure, has acquired the gift of self-awareness by magical means. Sentience is a boon for Maurice: he's able to perfect the feline art of manipulating others, and duly enlists a 'stupid-looking boy' and a troupe of intelligent rats in an elaborate Pied Piper scam. The changeling rats, who have taken names such as Peaches, Darktan, Dangerous Beans and Hamnpork ('the kind of name you give yourself if you learn to read before you understand what all the words actually mean'[59]), are becoming increasingly unhappy, however. They're sick of living by deception and want to make their own way in the world. Reluctantly, they agree to one last sting, in the town of Bad Blintz.

Now the rats are highly skilled operators. They have specialized Trap Disposal Squads and they're used to dealing with rat bait and poisons. They've learned to *think* their way through dangerous situations, and they have plans for the future, plans inspired in part by the vision of a better life contained in a little book which they've learned to revere: the enthralling *Mr Bunnsy Has an Adventure.*

Mr Bunnsy is a revelation and an enigma. The animals wear clothes and play tricks on each other, but no one ever comes to any real harm. Even more amazingly, the animals actually speak to humans, who treat them like smaller humans. What could *Mr Bunnsy* possibly mean? Who could have written it? And why? Surely no human could 'make a book about Ratty Rupert the rat, who wore a hat, *and* poison rats under the floorboards at the same time'[60]? No one can come up with a satisfactory answer, but they believe in the book all the same. With an eye on the future, the rats develop a canon of Thoughts to live by:

- In the Clan is Strength.
- We Co-operate, or we Die.
- Not to Widdle where you Eat.
- No Rat to Kill another Rat.

Since most of the clan still can't read Human, Peaches invents a written language they can all understand. Here is her translation of thought number four (the thick black line means 'no', and the trap represents 'bad' or 'die'):

Figure 24 From *The Amazing Maurice and His Educated Rodents* by Terry Pratchett, illustration by David Wyatt

It soon becomes apparent that something nasty is happening in Bad Blintz. There is a bounty on rat tails, and the *rathaus* has engaged a pair of rat-catchers who look like they enjoy their work. As Maurice and co. prepare to lay siege to the town, they meet the mayor's daughter, Malicia

Grim. Malicia is a reader and storyteller who is following in the footsteps of her forebears, the sisters Agoniza and Eviscera. She figures out the swindle in no time but appreciates the narrative force of the situation and throws in her lot with Maurice and the rats.

The rats explore the territory underground, sending their clockwork rat decoy, Mr Clicky, ahead to test the route. They proceed slowly, measuring every step, until at last they come upon a horrifying scene: hundreds of *keekees* (ordinary rats) crammed into cages. The rat-catchers are running their own scam, breeding rats for the lethal business of coursing. Hamnpork is captured; he's to fight Jacko the terrier in the pit that night.

Maurice helps the rats devise an escape plan. When the time comes, Sardines, a dancing rat who wears a small boater, will risk everything. That evening a crowd of men gather around the circle of death, cheering as Jacko the terrier begins his dreadful night's work. Hamnpork is released into the seething pit of rats. The crowd grows silent. Suddenly, a tiny figure sails through the air, string uncoiling behind him:

> [Sardines] came to a stop between the dog and the rat. For a moment he hung there. He raised his hat, politely, and said, 'Good evening!' Then he wrapped all four legs around Hamnpork … Too late, too late, Jacko snapped at empty air. The rats were accelerated upwards, out of the pit – and stopped, bouncing in mid air [61]

Once the rat-catchers have been exposed, other secrets come to light. The clan has been aware for some time that there is something else lurking deep underground, a malevolent voice that has been trying to mess with their minds. It's the voice of SPIDER, the rat king (an awful amalgam of individual rats twisted and tangled into one living entity), consumed by hatred for the humans who created it, and filled with contempt for any rat who dares to dream. He challenges Dangerous Beans:

> *'Oh, so you think you are a* good *rat? But a good rat is one that steals most! You think a good rat is a rat in a waistcoat, a little human with fur! Oh yes, I know about the stupid, stupid book! Traitor! Traitor to rats! Will you feel my … PAIN?'…*

> 'I am a rat,' whispered Dangerous Beans. 'But I am not vermin.'…

> *'THEN BE NOTHING!'*[62]

Maurice attacks but he cannot withstand the fury of the rat king. He falls, Dangerous Beans beside him. When DEATH appears to claim his due (his ratty offsider, the Bone Rat, at his side), Maurice trades one of his remaining lives to save his companion. ("'THAT IS VERY UN-CAT-LIKE OF YOU MAURICE. I'M AMAZED.' "I'm pretty shocked too, sir. I just hope no-one finds out, sir.'"[63])

In the town of Bad Blintz humans and rats find a way of coexisting peaceably, and Maurice moves on to another adventure.

The Amazing Maurice is a thoughtful story which shines with wry humor (Malicia is ashamed to admit that the cheese is 'only mousetrap'), dry wit (the 'doubting rat' is called Tomato), and slapstick ("'Went straight up your trouser legs, did they? Typical rat trick. Just nod, 'cos we don't want to set 'em off. No tellin' where it might end'"[64]). These light-hearted elements are offset by innovative linguistic playforms (written and spoken Rat, for example, or cat curses in the original Cat and in translation) and intertextual puzzles which call for risky, what-if thinking.

Intertextual play with perspective permeates every aspect of the text. Beginning with *Mr Bunnsy Has an Adventure*, the curious intratextual story which introduces each chapter, the intertexts are so densely layered that it is a challenge to identify them all.

Mr Bunnsy is a strange little fiction which manages to be arch *and* sentimental at the same time. A parody of Beatrix Potter's talking animal stories, with a touch of *The Wind in The Willows*, Rupert Bear, *The Runaway Bunny* and Aesop's Fables thrown in for good measure, *Mr Bunnsy* makes for uncomfortable reading – it is absurd ('Mr Bunnsy had a lot of friends in Furry Bottom') but unnerving ('Never go into the Dark Wood … There are bad things in there.').

We're inclined to laugh when the changelings are taken in by this preposterous tale. It's ridiculous: 'there's no subtext, no social commentary,' Malicia Grim scoffs. But is she correct? As it happens, anthropomorphic animal stories such as *The Tale of Peter Rabbit* were not at all sentimental when it came to the subject of animal welfare. Peter's father ended up in a pie, and Peter very nearly met the same fate. Waistcoats and pinafores notwithstanding, Beatrix Potter had a staunch animal protection message for her readers. Seen from this perspective, *Peter Rabbit's* successor *Mr Bunnsy* might not be as silly as it seems. Either way, it proves to be a source of useful ideas which the rats can adapt for practical purposes. Where would the Trap Disposal Squad be without their belts and pockets?

Mr Bunnsy is another *mise en abyme*, a story within a story which encapsulates the entire narrative in miniature. Web users might call it a meme, a replica or imitation which retains something of the original image but spins off on a life of its own. These patterns abound in *The Amazing Maurice*. Let's take a look at the suite of multidimensional perspectives associated with the rat clan.

The changelings are rats with personality. They are fascinating characters: witty, courageous, and optimistic. They have learned that co-operation is important, so they respect each other and work together for a bright, ratty future. Now flip the image. What comes into focus? SPIDER the rat-king, a dark star of rats tied together for all time. Unlike the changelings, who came into being serendipitously, the rat king was fashioned by men for their own purposes. The rat clan is a group of individuals; the rat king is a fabrication, a figure of urban myth and folklore, and a living *thing*. Seen from a slightly different point of view, the rat king is also a terrible caricature of Mr Clicky, the clockwork rat who bumps along with a candle burning on his back. Mr Clicky is an object too, a cat toy set to work by the rats. He's a useful creature, valuable but expendable, easily replaced by another Mr Clicky when he needs to be.

The rat clan perspectives converge to remind us what can happen when empathy fails and people treat others (humans and other living creatures) as if they were objects. In the end, it's the capacity to see the world as others see it that triumphs. The rats reject the utopian premise of *Mr Bunnsy*, but find something akin to it: a way of living which appreciates different points of view:

> A man was painting, very carefully, a little picture underneath the street sign that said 'River Street'. It was a long way underneath, only just higher than the pavement, and he had to kneel down. He kept referring to a small piece of paper in his hand …

Figure 25 From *The Amazing Maurice and His Educated Rodents* by Terry Pratchett, illustration by David Wyatt

'It's in the Rat alphabet … It says Water+Fast+Stones. The streets have got cobbles on, right? So the rats see them as stones. It means River Street.'[65]

I can think of no better place to conclude this discussion of textual playfulness. In the final chapter I will look at different ways of sharing the texts with children.

Notes

1   Russell Hoban, *The Mouse and His Child*, illustrated by Lillian Hoban (London: Faber and Faber, 2000), 2; illustrated by David Small (New York: Arthur A. Levine Books, 2001), 3. *The Mouse and His Child* was first published in 1967.

2   David Lewis, 'The constructedness of texts: picture books and the metafictive,' *Signal* 62 (May 1990), 131.

3   See Lois Rostow Kuznets, *When Toys Come Alive: Narratives of Animation, Metamorphosis and Development* (New Haven, CT: Yale University Press, 1994) for more on this intriguing subject.

4   This aspect of word and image interaction is discussed in Perry Nodelman, *The Pleasures of Children's Literature* (New York: Longman, 1992), 157.

5   Margaret Meek, *How Texts Teach What Readers Learn* (Stroud, UK: The Thimble Press, 1988), 18.

6   Lisa S. Ede, citing the work of the play theorist Eugene Fink, remarks on this phenomenon in 'An introduction to the nonsense literature of Edward Lear and Lewis Carroll,' in *Explorations in the Field of Nonsense*, ed. Wim Tigges (Amsterdam: Rodopi, 1987), 59.

    For a useful overview of this motif in children's fiction see Robyn McCallum, 'Very advanced texts: metafictions and experimental work,' in *Understanding Children's Literature: Key Essays from the International Encyclopedia of Children's Literature*, ed. Peter Hunt (London: Routledge, 1999), 146–147.

7   See Geoffrey Williams, 'Children entering literate worlds: perspectives from the study of textual practices,' in *Literacy and Schooling*, edited by Frances Christie and Ray Misson (London: Routledge, 1998), 21.

8   Philip Nel's video presentation, *Metafiction for Children*, is an excellent introduction to the subject. Retrieved on 28 June 2014 from www.philnel. com/2010/09/04/more-metafiction/

9   Tove Jansson, *The Book about Moomin, Mymble and Little My* (Helsinki: Holger Schildts Förlag, 1952). English translation by Sophie Hannah (London: Sort of Books, 2001), opening 7.

10 Nel, *Metafiction for Children*.

11 As described by Holly Giffin in 'The coordination of meaning in the creation of a shared make-believe reality,' in *Symbolic Play: The Development of Social Understanding*, ed. Inge Bretherton (Orlando, FL: Academic Press, 1984), 82–84. Also see the discussion by Bretherton in the same volume, 'Representing the social world in symbolic play,' 28.

12 Other metacommunicative options include enactment, covert conversation, storytelling, prompting, and formal pretend proposals. For further detail, see Giffin, 'The coordination of meaning,' 79–88.

13 Ibid., 84.

14 McCallum, 'Very advanced texts: metafictions and experimental work,' 138–150.

15 See Gérard Genette, 'Voice' in *Narratology: An Introduction*, ed. Susana Onega and José Angel García Landa (London: Longman, 1996), 173–189.

    Narrative has several dimensions. As Genette (ibid.) explains, the *extradiegetic* level is outside the fictional world; this is the realm of the narrator who is separate from the story he or she is telling. The *diegetic* level refers to the world of the characters – it is their story which the narrator relates. The *metadiegetic* or *hypodiegetic* refers to an embedded level – to narrative in the second degree. Robyn McCallum describes the process of narrative frame breaking more fully: 'Metaleptic disruptions to the diegetic level of narration breach conventional relationships and hierarchies between characters, texts, authors, illustrators and readers.' Robyn McCallum, 'Would I lie to you? Metalepsis and modal disruption in some "true" fairy tales,' in *Postmodern Picturebooks: Play, Parody and Self-Referentiality*, eds. Lawrence R. Sipe and Sylvia Pantaleo (New York: Routledge, 2008), 181.

16 David Lewis, *Reading Contemporary Picturebooks: Picturing Text* (London: Routledge/Falmer, 2001), 85.

17 Joanna Carey, 'Bruce Ingman: the line of beauty,' *The Guardian*, Saturday 20 June 2009. Retrieved on 28 June 2014 from www.theguardian.co.uk/books/2009/jun/20/bruce-ingham (this is the correct URL despite the misspelling of 'Ingman' at the end).

18 David Macaulay, *Black and White* (Boston, MA: Houghton Mifflin Company, 1990; London: Hodder and Stoughton, 1990).

19 For a persuasive reading of the text, see Michele Anstey, '"It's not all black and white": postmodern picture books and new literacies,' *Journal of Adolescent and Adult Literacy* 45(6) (2002), 444–458.

20 As discussed by Dudley Jones in 'Only make-believe? Lies, fictions, and metafictions in Geraldine McCaughrean's *A Pack of Lies* and Philip Pullman's *Clockwork*,' *The Lion and the Unicorn* 23(1) (1999), 86–96.

21 In fact, there is an interesting example of inverse parallelism between Edgar Allan Poe's experiences with the publishing world and 'Harris Burdick's' encounter with the publisher, 'Peter Wenders'. Just before his death, Poe revised his stories and left them in the care of his literary executor, Rufus W. Griswold. Griswold is said to have repaid him by printing a defamatory obituary and making alterations to the manuscripts which he subsequently published.

22 Aidan Chambers, 'Ways of telling: from writer to reader: An author reads himself', in *Booktalk: Occasional Writing on Literature and Children* (London: Bodley Head, 1985; Woodchester: The Thimble Press, 1995), 102.

23 *Through the Looking Glass*. Chambers remarks on the connection in 'Ways of telling', 103.

24 Lauren Child, *Ruby Redfort: Look Into My Eyes* (London: HarperCollins Children's Books, 2011. Somerville, MA: Candlewick Press, 2012). This is the first book in the *Ruby Redfort* series.

25 Freud's celebrated essay 'The uncanny' offers a close reading of 'The Sandman'; see Sigmund Freud, 'The uncanny', in *Art and Literature*, ed. Albert Dickson, trans. James Strachey, The Penguin Freud Library vol. 14 (Harmondsworth: Penguin Books, 1990), 339–376.

    Other Hoffmann stories which focus on machine animation and toys coming alive include 'Automata' and 'Nutcracker and the King of Mice'. See E. T. A. Hoffmann, *The Best Tales of Hoffmann*, ed. E. F. Bleiler (New York: Dover Publications, 1967).

26 Jones, 'Only make-believe?', 92.

27 Bette Goldstone, 'The paradox of space in postmodern picturebooks', in Sipe and Pantaleo, *Postmodern Picturebooks*, 120.

28 For more on the 'shared secret of what is really going on beneath the water', see David Wiesner's audio file 'What is *flotsam*?' posted on 17 August 2006 and retrieved on 28 June 2014 from www.thefishknowthesecret.com/logs

29 Pioneered by Hergé (Georges Remi) in his *Tintin* comics.

30 This response by a fifth-grade reader is cited in Sylvia Pantaleo's study, '"How could that be?": Reading Banyai's *Zoom* and *Re-Zoom*', *Language Arts* 84(3) (2007), 228.

31 The term *mise en abyme* was coined by André Gide, who compared it to a heraldic device where the image of a shield is depicted containing, at its center, a miniature replica of itself.

    My analysis of the *mise en abyme* is informed by Lucien Dällenbach's exhaustive study of *mises en abyme* and reflexivity, *The Mirror in the Text*, trans. Jeremy Whiteley with Emma Hughes (Cambridge: Polity Press, 1989). While the *mise en abyme* is difficult to define, Dällenbach introduces the concept this way: 'the *mise en abyme*, as a means by which the work turns back on itself, appears to be a kind of *reflexion*. [I]ts essential property is that it brings out the meaning and form of the work' (p. 8). Later, he identifies 'two factors that determine the emergence of the device: (i) the reflexion of the whole of the narrative in one or other of its major elements; and (ii) the diegetic or metadiegetic [hypodiegetic] status of this reflexion' (p. 137).

32 As noted in Chapter 2, *ilinx* is one of the four categories of play. Its textual application is discussed at some length by Iser in *The Fictive and the Imaginary: Charting Literary Anthropology* (Baltimore, MD: The Johns Hopkins University Press, 1993), 258–272.

33 Norton Juster, *The Phantom Tollbooth*, illustrated by Jules Feiffer (London: Collins, 1974), 161–162; (New York: Yearling), 191.

34 Hoban, *The Mouse and His Child*, Faber and Faber edition, 19–20 et passim; Arthur A. Levine edition, 29–30 et passim.

35 Ibid., Faber, 17; Levine, 27.

36 Ibid., Faber, 148; Levine, 220.

37 'The Clock', in Russell Hoban, *La Corona and the Tin Frog*, illustrated by Nicola Bayley (London: Jonathan Cape, 1979; New York: Smithmark Publishers, 1987), final unnumbered page.

38 Hoban, *The Mouse and His Child*, Faber, 165; Levine, 244.

39 From Margaret S. Libby's review of *The Cat in the Hat* published in the *New York Herald Tribune Book Review* and cited by Philip Nel in *The Annotated Cat: Under the Hats of Seuss and His Cats* (New York: Random House, 2007), 10.

40 A. O. Scott, 'Sense and nonsense', *New York Times Magazine*, 26 November 2000.

41 Juster, *The Phantom Tollbooth*, Collins edition, 34–35; Yearling edition, 38–40.

42 David Wiesner used the cryptographic device known as a Cardan Grille to construct his faux scientific language. 'I drew up a collection of 30 or so symbols to define my language and put them into a grid. I then made a template with three open windows. I placed it over the grid, writing down the symbols that appeared in the windows. I then turned the template 90 degrees and wrote down the next set of symbols and so on. This way characters will recur, but randomly'. Retrieved on 28 June 2014 from www.davidwiesner.com/work/say-what/

43 Hoban, *The Mouse and His Child*, Faber, 6; Levine, 7–8.

44 Juster, *The Phantom Tollbooth*, Collins, 69; Yearling, 79.

45 Michael Hall, *My Heart Is Like a Zoo* (New York: Greenwillow Books, 2010), openings 1, 4, 6, 7.

46 As discussed by the author in 'A conversation with Michael Hall' in *A Reading and Discussion Guide* prepared by The Minnesota Book Awards and The Friends of the Saint Paul Public Library. The guide was retrieved on 28 June

2014 from http://thefriends.org/wp-content/uploads/2012/12/my-heart-is-like-a-zoo.pdf

47 Lauren Child, *I Will Not Ever Never Eat a Tomato* (London: Orchard Books, 2000; Somerville, MA: Candlewick Press, 2003), opening 16.

48 Janet and Allan Ahlberg, *The Worm Book* (Harmondsworth and New York: Puffin Books, 2000), unnumbered page 1.

49 Ibid., unnumbered page 17.

50 Hoban, *The Mouse and His Child*, Faber, 71; Levine, 108–109.

51 Jon Scieszka and Daniel Adel, *The Book That Jack Wrote* (New York: Viking, 1994; Harmondsworth: Puffin Books, 1999).

52 Shaun Tan's description, from his website: www.shauntan.net/books.html. Retrieved on 28 June 2014.

53 John Stephens, '"They are always surprised at what people throw away": glocal postmodernism in Australian picturebooks', in Sipe and Pantaleo, *Postmodern Picturebooks*, 94–96.

54 See Tony Watkins and Zena Sutherland, 'Contemporary children's literature (1970–present)', in *Children's Literature: An Illustrated History*, ed. Peter Hunt (Oxford: Oxford University Press, 1995), 314.

55 Janet and Allan Ahlberg, *The Jolly Pocket Postman* (London: William Heinemann, 1995; New York: Little, Brown and Company, 1995), insert at opening 9 (in both editions).

56 Ibid., insert at opening 15 (both editions).

57 From an interview with Anthony Browne in 2004 cited by the online database TeachingBooks.net. Retrieved on 28 June 2014 from www.teachingbooks.net/content/Browne_qu.pdf

58 Population: 21 pairs.

59 Terry Pratchett, *The Amazing Maurice and His Educated Rodents*, illustrated by David Wyatt (London: Corgi Books, 2002), 24; (New York: HarperCollins, 2008), 21. The HarperCollins edition reads: 'the kind of name you gave yourself if you learned to read before you understood what the words actually meant'.

60 Ibid., Corgi edition, 48; HarperCollins edition, 51.

61 Ibid., Corgi, 156–157; HarperCollins, 190.

62 Ibid., Corgi, 209, 211; HarperCollins, 261, 263, 264. The HarperCollins edition reads: 'a rat in a vest …'.

63 Ibid., Corgi, 221; HarperCollins, 276.

64 Ibid., Corgi, 15; HarperCollins, 8.

65 Ibid., Corgi, 266–267; HarperCollins, 335–336.

6 Learning to look: reading playful texts with children

> It was as though the whole world broke down into pieces so that I could look into it. It was as though the whole world froze for that one glimpse.
>
> Ethan, reading Istvan Banyai's *Zoom*[1]

6.1 Orientation

As I have argued throughout this book, playful texts – self-reflexive texts which adopt the perspective-taking measures of pretend play – ask readers to explore different viewpoints and take an active role in the connection-making game that makes the story run. These texts have something to offer everyone. They yield more with each reading and generate different meanings for different readers. They appeal to varied age groups, offer multiple reading paths (think of the reversible texts we've discussed so far, and all of the open-ended stories, *mises en abyme* and fictional worlds within worlds), incorporate a polyphony of textual and intertextual narrative voices, and encourage readers to look deeply, beneath the surface of things.

While playful texts take pains to foreground sense-making devices (they have to do this: foregrounding is integral to their playfulness), readers need to pay attention to subtleties and look for verbal and visual clues at work in the text. There are various age-appropriate strategies which can be used by parents and teachers to encourage children to analyze illustrations, recognize verbal and visual playfulness, build on previous real-world and reading experiences, appreciate different narrative styles and techniques, and share their observations with others.[2] Before introducing these shared-reading strategies, it may be useful to revise the key textual features that are likely to come into play when reading and discussing the texts with children.[3] Some elements will be more appropriate than others depending on context. Shared reading at school is obviously a very different experience from bed time reading with an adult at home.

Textual features

First impressions:

- Size and shape of the book.
- Page layout.
- Physical qualities and fabric (pop-ups, fold-outs and die-cuts).
- Multimodality. Words and images have a symbiotic relationship in picturebooks. They may complement, extend or contradict one another. Occasionally words and images merge to create unique semiotic playforms.

Illustrations:

- Mood and atmosphere.
- Color: hues, shades and saturation.
- Tone and texture.
- Contour, shape and line. Framing, shading, blurring, hatching, cross-hatching and stippling.
- Location of figures on the page.
- Dimension: foreground, middle ground and background.
- Focus: close-ups, mid-focus, long distance.
- Angles: frontal, side-on, high and low.
- Perspective and vectors (establishing connections between characters).
- Gestures, facial expressions and body language.
- The relationship between the reader and the text: point of view (where the reader stands); proximity (the distance between the reader and the text); communication between a character and the reader (direct or averted gaze).
- Visual symbols, metaphors, jokes and nonsense.
- Other graphic features such as maps, charts, diagrams and tables.
- Media.
- Techniques such as collage and photomontage.
- Cultural references, art movements and styles of individual artists.
- Intertextual allusions.

Written text:

- Form: fairy tale (or fractured fairy tale), folk tale, fable, allegory, novel, graphic novel, short story, play, poem.
- Genre: fantasy, science fiction, adventure story, mystery, historical fiction.
- Setting.
- Characters and narrator(s).
- Story, plot and discourse (as appropriate).
- Point of view (as appropriate for older readers).
- Structure (including playful structures such as the *mise en abyme*).
- Sound devices: rhythm, meter, rhyme, other forms of repetition (including alliteration and assonance), onomatopoeia.
- Figurative language: imagery, symbol, metaphor, simile, hyperbole, personification, synecdoche, metonymy, paradox, irony.
- Intertextual allusions.
- Typeface, font, and layout.

6.2 Shared-reading strategies

We have established that reading is an interactive process, with children learning to read in partnership with other readers and with the text itself. As discussed in Chapter 4, more experienced readers support the reading experience in various ways, encouraging beginners to build on what they already know and urging them to glean new meanings from the text they are reading together. In this section, I will focus on a number of scaffolding strategies which have proved to be effective when introducing playful picturebooks to young readers.

The picture walk

Very young children can learn a great deal from taking a picture walk[4] with a co-reader. Focusing on the cover and the illustrations before reading the story aloud, the aim is to encourage children to look closely at the images on the page, talk about what they see, and make predictions about what might be happening in the story as a whole. This suspense-building exercise ('Have you seen anything like that before?' 'What's happening in the background?' 'How do you think the story will end?') gives young readers the chance to practice inference-making skills while they are learning to interpret images. It's also fun to test the accuracy of predictions.

As proponents have pointed out, picture walks can be particularly helpful for teachers working with English language learners and children from varied backgrounds. 'The picture walk can help an adult reader meet students where they are, and she can also use the illustrations to help students learn vocabulary and visualize experiences they have not yet had themselves.'[5]

What do I *See*? What do I *Think*? What do I *Wonder*?

The next strategy – What do I *See*? What do I *Think*? What do I *Wonder*? (STW)[6] – requires readers to pay attention to subtle aspects of illustrations (slight changes in facial expressions, unusual angles, odd placement of images, mixed media and visual puns) which might otherwise be overlooked. This speculative approach stimulates curiosity, promotes what-if thinking, and gives young readers opportunities to engage with other people's opinions.

To present the strategy for the first time, choose a picturebook with a striking front cover. *Chester* by Mélanie Watt should work well. The page is dominated by a fat tabby cat gazing directly at the reader, an exceedingly self-satisfied expression on his face. He is clutching a large red marker in one paw, and the angle of the marker creates a direct link (or vector) with a red sticker-shaped sign which reads: 'Place my award here.' The title is emblazoned across the top of the page and at the bottom the author's name has been crossed out and replaced by 'Chester' in bold red letters. In the far left-hand corner we can see that Chester is sitting on a tiny white mouse which is struggling to get away. The mouse is actually looking in two directions at once – one eye is searching for an escape route off the page to the left, and the other is gazing angrily at the viewer, possibly appealing for help.

To begin, invite the children to participate by asking them to look carefully at the cover. Emphasize that they are going to learn a new way of looking at illustrations in picturebooks. Like detectives, they will be able to interpret clues hidden in the pictures. They will also discover that words *and* pictures count in telling the story.

Next, focus on a single element of the illustration and model the strategy:

- 'I *see* that Mélanie Watt's name has been replaced with Chester's.'
- 'I *think* I know who might have done it. What clues can you find?'
- 'I *wonder* how Mélanie Watt must feel.'

This should be enough to generate spirited conversation and debate. Children who've encountered Chester in other books will have much to contribute, as will those who have additional theories about the missing sticker and the disorientated mouse.

Repeat the STW process each time a new book is introduced. When children are familiar with the strategy, ask them to practice with a partner. The exercise can be extended by encouraging children to draw their own illustrations.

Booktalk with older readers

Older readers generally need less structured reading strategies. Teachers often adopt a workshop approach, reading aloud to students and organizing whole-class and literature study group discussions, focusing perhaps on a particular genre, theme or author.[7] The key is to create an appropriate setting – at home or at school – where teachers and more experienced readers can scaffold sense-making procedures, and where children can take the time they need to focus closely on illustrations and written text, ask questions, try out different meanings, share their interpretations with other children and adults, and create texts of their own.

Aidan Chambers has developed a collaborative approach for encouraging 'booktalk' and critical thinking. His 'Tell me' framework[8] starts with four basic questions:

- Is there anything you like about the book?
- Is there anything you dislike?
- Is there anything you find puzzling?
- Do you notice any patterns, any connections in the book? (This may involve identifying one or two key elements that form part of a narrative pattern and inviting readers to find other elements.)

Once children are comfortable discussing their initial impressions, adults can elicit more detailed responses, using general questions such as these:

*Tell me ... When you first saw the book, even before you read it, what
kind of book did you think it was going to be?*
Can you tell me what made you think this?
Now you've read it, is it as you expected?

Have you read this book before? [If so:] Was it different this time?
Did you notice anything this time you didn't notice before?
Did you enjoy it more or less?
*Because of what happened to you when reading it again, would you
recommend other people to read it more than once, or isn't it worth it?*

Specific questions can then be used to develop critical skills:

How long did it take for the story to happen?
Did we find out about the story in the order in which things happened?
*When you talk about things that happen to you, do you always tell your
story in the order in which they happened? Or are there sometimes reasons why you don't? What are the reasons?*

*Who was telling – who was narrating – the story? Do we know? How do
we know?*

*Did we ever get to know what the characters were thinking about? Were
we told what they were feeling? Or was the story told all the time from
outside the characters, watching what they did and hearing what they
said, but never knowing what they were thinking or feeling?*

Chambers offers 21 possible questions, emphasizing that some will
obviously be more relevant than others in any reading group.

Our experience of using the 'Tell me' approach is that after a while the
Framework sinks into the back of the mind; then we don't consciously use
it. We begin to listen more attentively to the questions children generate
themselves – and use those as springboards.[9]

6.3 Children interacting with playful texts

It is now time to listen to the children themselves. The case studies reproduced below involve young readers of various ages (six-12 years) and
reading abilities interacting with playful picturebooks in British, Australian
and US classrooms. These studies, the first of which was conducted more
than 25 years ago, show young children building visual literacy and metalinguistic awareness, negotiating complex sense-making procedures, and
reveling in narrative play. They are a revelation.

Abdullah and Mark: learning to read with *Bear Hunt* (Australia)

Working with very inexperienced readers in the later years of primary
school whose previous reading education had consisted of memorizing iso-
lated words on flash cards, Geoff Williams and David Jack created a playful
visual environment for their students, cleared out all reading scheme material, and placed narrative at the center of all that they sought to achieve in
reading sessions.[10] Playful picturebooks proved to be particularly effective:

> Abdullah and Mark H. taught us through their interest in *Bear Hunt*.
> Abdullah's enthusiasm for the book was so great we asked him as a
> 'retelling activity' to make his own version by drawing his own pictures
> to accompany the original text. He worked on this activity for many days,
> delighting in his ability to read a book for the first time in his life.
>
> Mark H. perhaps caught some of Abdullah's enthusiasm. David's diary
> entry notes from this period are instructive:
>
> > *Mark H. was very keen to write a sequel to* Bear Hunt. *He asked me*
> > *on a number of occasions if he could do this. Before this time Mark*
> > *had rarely shown an interest in books, preferring to state his inability*
> > *to read and thus not complete any of the required reading tasks. Now*
> > *having completed his 'book' he is able to reconstruct his story without*
> > *any concrete aid.*
>
> In Mark's case the original was not used. He began with Anthony
> Browne's narrative but transformed it, working with Mark N. and Scott,
> into a different story. What was so remarkable to us was his playfulness
> with the original narrative given his almost total lack of interest in written
> language at the beginning of the year.[11]

This assessment is significant on several counts. It shows how appropriate books can transform non-readers into enthusiasts, and it highlights the ways in which active reading can generate confidence, curiosity and perseverance. Abdullah was so elated by his success with *Bear Hunt* that he subsequently wrote to Anthony Browne, highlighting what he liked about the text and asking for a sequel. This represented another major breakthrough for Abdullah, whose writing up to that point had been limited to single sentence narratives written by teachers on his behalf.

Equally important is the way Abdullah's encounter with *Bear Hunt* inspired the other students, not only motivating them to write their own stories, but also encouraging them to do so in a playful, collaborative manner. Ultimately the boys managed both to interrogate and to transform the original text, investing it with a new set of meanings while simultaneously reconstructing their view of themselves as readers.

By the end of the year, the nature and status of written text had radically changed for the children who worked with Williams and Jack. The extensive use of playful narratives, and play with those narratives, had clearly contributed to this breakthrough. As the teachers observed,

> [p]lay around and in the stories ... was important for the development of a sense of [empowerment]. It was a form of joint celebration of stories in which we could all participate and which helped build up sets of shared understandings in the group.[12]

The selection of narratives incorporating textual puzzles, visual nonsense and language games was considered to be significant. So was the fact that the narrators of these stories show more than they tell explicitly, making room for the reader's input. In the special case of *Bear Hunt*, the boys participated in the metafictive play of the text, extending its meaning and creating their own narratives as they proceeded.

When they were encouraged to discuss what they had read, Abdullah and his classmates readily identified contradictions between the written text and the illustrations. They had no problem dealing with ambiguity, and appeared to welcome it.[13] They were not sophisticated readers but they delighted in the opportunity to engage in narrative play and to question the ways texts make meaning.

Time to Get Out of the Bath, Shirley: two readings (UK)

As discussed in Chapter 5, John Burningham's *Time to Get Out of the Bath, Shirley* is an imaginative text which inscribes the operations of make-believe play in a way that requires the reader to negotiate what appear to be two very different stories, as well as two distinctive modes of narration, in the same narrative. In *Reading Contemporary Picturebooks: Picturing Text*, David Lewis discusses the intricacies of the text with two six-year-old readers, Nathan and Jane.

> Nathan and Jane make an interesting contrast as readers of Burningham. Nathan – the weaker reader in terms of his decoding skills – makes a more sophisticated reader of the text than Jane, who is puzzled by the fact that Shirley's mum does not seem to be able to see that her daughter has slipped down the plughole.[14]

> In Nathan's case it was not the same story at the beginning, or even halfway through, as it was at the end. It is clear from the transcript of our conversation that Nathan held the story in suspension as we read together and he attempted to sort out what was going on.[15]

> [At this point Shirley's mother can be seen [on the left-hand side of the double-page spread] mopping up splashes on the bathroom floor while over on the right-hand side Shirley is engaged in a mock joust with the king and has just knocked him off his mount.]

> N: (exclaims) She punches the king in!
> DL: Hmm ... NOW THERE'S WATER EVERYWHERE!
>
> N: 'Cos she's punched the king in.
> DL: Why? What do you mean?
> N: She punched the king in and it probably made a splash ... She's probably still playing in the bath.
> DL: Yes? You mean the king falling in the water ... what that's done?
> N: Yes. She's playing with her toys.
> DL: Ah. I see. So you don't think this is a real king then?
> N: No.
> DL: No?
> N: It's just a toy ...
> DL: Oh I see. So what about all this galloping about on horseback?
> N: She was probably using her fingers.
> DL: Using her ... how would she use her fingers?

N: Like ... going like that (making two fingers gallop like legs) ... and putting little people on her fingers.[16]

For Jane, the moment of revelation came only at the very end after she had finished. In her case, she appears to have read two stories. There is the one that took shape as she was reading about a little girl who slips down the plughole of her bath in much the same way as Alice goes down the rabbit hole, and who meets strange characters rather like Alice does. And then there is the one that dawned on her later when she had finished and had been prompted by me (I asked her 'do you think she's really gone down the plughole?' to which she replied, very quietly, 'No, I think she's only dreaming or something.') In neither case – Nathan's or Jane's – is this a simple matter of making an interpretation of events, something that can clearly be done long after the story has taken place, as both children were concerned to establish what the events were in the first place.[17]

We can see that both children learned a valuable reading lesson through their interaction with the text. They were transformed as readers, and they transformed the text in the process, clearly contributing something to the story 'not present in Burningham's pictures and words.'[18]

First-grade children read Wiesner's *The Three Pigs* (US)

This study, conducted by Lawrence Sipe,[19] highlights the way that young readers (six to seven year olds) can, in the right circumstances and in the company of the right text, tolerate uncertainty and cope with moments of cognitive dissonance.

The reading session took the form of a read-aloud by a visiting teacher. The children were familiar with traditional storytelling conventions and had, in the weeks leading up to the case study, listened to many other versions of The Three Pigs story.

Accustomed to responding to texts in read-aloud groups, the children were quick to comment on the lifelike appearance of the pigs on the cover. Their intertextual knowledge informed this interesting exchange:

STEVEN: *The Three Grownup Pigs.*
NATHAN: They're real pigs.
NORMAN: They're, they look like *real* three pigs. And in the other stories, the other pigs didn't really look a lot like pigs.

Morgan: They're pigs like animal pigs and the other ones are like people
              pigs …
Nathan: These [gesturing toward the front dust jacket cover] are going to
              die.[20]

The children followed along until the moment when the first little pig encounters the wolf. They knew very well that the wolf huffed, and puffed, till he blew the house down and ate the pig up. There's no problem with the written text: that's exactly what it says. However, they could see the little pig flying off the page and announcing, 'Hey! He blew me right out of the story!'

At this point the children were very confused, and tried their best to reconcile the clear contradiction between the words, 'and ate the pig up' with the illustration, which shows the pig – very much alive – and the confused wolf, surrounded by the shattered remnants of the straw house …

Mandy: How does he eat him up?
Dominique: [in a wondering tone] He blew him out of the story.
Steven: Maybe he jumped out of the story with him and ate him.
Tim: Maybe the wolf's looking for him.
Dominique: No.
Alex: And *then* he ate him up.
Dominique: Pretend he was, maybe he was just joking that he ate him up.
Alex: Maybe he thought when he blew the house down he might
               have ate a lot of straw and *thought* he ate the pig.[21]

As discussed in Chapter 5, the fairy tale text struggles to stick to its script while the pigs all escape into a metafictive dimension beyond the story. There they make a paper plane out of the pages of 'The Three Pigs' (the children were so transfixed by this feat that they managed to spot tiny pieces of the wolf on and under the wings) and fly off into blank, white space. Where are they going?

Dominique: Maybe to the trash.
Melanie: It's not over yet.
Keith: Maybe the plane will go out of control and go back to another
               script and the story will continue.
Martin: They're still flying.

ANTHONY:	There's his [the wolf's] leg again.
STEVEN:	It's just a piece of paper.
ALEX:	Maybe the airplane is going to fly into the trash and there will be this white paper and the pigs will be out.
TEACHER:	They are going to escape forever? No more three little pigs' stories?
DOMINIQUE AND MANDY:	[Gasp!][22]

When the pigs eventually come to land they find themselves in a weird intertextual space populated by nursery rhyme characters which look oddly familiar. The children took this in their stride.

KEITH:	I bet they're in another story.
MANDY:	Another three pigs.
STEVEN:	No more three pigs!
MANDY:	It might be another three little pigs story.
MELANIE:	And then they meet themselves.[23]

As in the case of *Bear Hunt* above, the children responded to the radical playfulness of *The Three Pigs* and enjoyed its many challenges. As readers, they learned to appreciate the deviations in the plot, helped each other keep track of the characters' bewildering transformations, and 'interpreted the liminal space *between* stories in a remarkably sophisticated way.'[24] And all this in a *first* reading! In the next study, we will see what can be achieved with multiple readings of a polyphonic text.

Responding to *Voices in the Park* (US)

In this study, a group of 20 eight to twelve year olds read *Voices in the Park* in a literature workshop. The evaluation was conducted by Frank Serafini.[25]

The children had been in a multi-age classroom setting for one, two or three years … Anthony Browne's text was used as a cornerstone text … meaning this book was read and discussed in depth over several days before introducing any of the other books in the unit of study.

The first reading … introduced readers to the story and provided opportunities for initial responses and discussion. The second reading of the story was done the next day and involved the whole class and small group discussions. Classroom wall charts were used to preserve and represent readers' interpretations of the text and illustrations ... The third reading focused on a teacher designed version of the book ... on several sheets of paper, keeping the line breaks consistent with the original text, but leaving out the illustrations. The final reading focused on the illustrations alone. The teacher made color copies of the entire book and displayed the book in storyboard fashion on a wall in the classroom ... Students wrote each day in their individual literature response logs and in a community literature response log called their walking journal.[26]

As the extracts from their conversations reveal, the children focused on three particular aspects of the text: its nonlinear structure, the relationship between word and image, and the use of visual symbolism.

Preliminary discussions concentrated on the unusual structure of the book. The children were challenged by the fact that they needed to make sense of four separate narratives:

TEACHER: Did you notice anything about the way the book was organized?

CATHY: Like how there were four stories, and not just one?

ADAM: I liked how one person told their story, and time went by. And then, the time would go back for the next voice to say what they wanted to say.

CARSON: That was weird, and I didn't get it at first.

TEACHER: Even though the voices were in order, First-Second-Third-Fourth Voice, they were all taking place at the same time.

CATHY: All the voices were happening at the same time, but just in a different place.

SHANNON: It was like a circular story for each voice. They always came to the park and they always left the park ...[27]

The next day the teacher read the book a second time. Why, a number of students wondered, had Anthony Browne bothered with the written text?

ANDREW: Because it's like a person went to the park and had a good time, a person went to the park trying to find a job, a person went to the park and had to yell at her kid and dog? Why even put text to it?

TEACHER: So you think the pictures told the story?

ANDREW: Better than the text did.

CARSON: It would have been better just as a picture book with no words.[28]

An alternative viewpoint emerged, however, acknowledging the role of the written text and the sense-making cues provided by its four clearly differentiated typefaces and fonts.

> BRITTNEY: Just thinking about it ... *the pictures don't tell what the text is doing.* [They] just *show*, like the background could be gloomy. That's only the mood, it's not like what is going on ... [T]he voices without the text ... wouldn't explain the characters ... I can picture the characters because of the font and the voice.[29]

The children grappled with these issues, discovering in the process that the overall meaning of the text is greater than the sum of its (verbal and visual) parts – particularly when visual symbols and other playful forms are used to create new worlds of meaning. In the following conversation, the children demonstrated a real understanding of symbolic representation.

> ANGELA: I noticed that all of the pictures have something weird going on ...
>
> CATHY: I noticed that in the back [background] the trees were really colourful. When everyone was happy, he [Browne] lightened up the colors of the pictures. When it got a little sadder, the pictures got dark.
>
> SALLY: Then, when you look at the pictures you see the different things going on. When I saw the trees blowing, it's kind of like mocking or making fun of [the mother]. Just joking around.
>
> ALLISON: I notice that for every separate voice, the trees and the season is different ...
>
> TEACHER: Good ideas ... Eric, share with us what you're thinking about the dogs.
>
> ERIC: The whole story revolves around the dogs, because you have for every voice, it shows them walking to the park. They wouldn't be able to have all those voices if they didn't have the dogs, they wouldn't have gone to the park.
>
> TEACHER: I agree. I hadn't put it into words. But, I agree that the story really revolves around the dogs.
>
> BRITTNEY: [I]n the picture I noticed, there's always something dividing them except for the dogs, so it kind of symbolizes them ... being one and showing them it doesn't really matter ... if he's rich and she's poor.[30]

Engaging with wordless texts: students read *Zoom* (US)

We have established that it is the interplay of word and image, written text and illustrations, which distinguishes a picturebook from an illustrated story. There is only one exception to this rule: a visual text or wordless picturebook. In that case, the verbal text is left entirely up to the reader. In the following case study, Sylvia Pantaleo charts the journey taken by a group of 5th grade students reading the visual texts, *Zoom* and *Re-Zoom*. The extracts reproduced here focus exclusively on *Zoom*.

As explained previously, the imaginary camera in *Zoom* zooms out, shot by shot, revealing more and more objects in each frame. Banyai's visual sleight-of-hand is highly accomplished. As his superimposed pictures multiply, focal points shift and the field of vision enlarges to encompass other images (and other embedded/interconnected stories). Here's what the children had to say after several readings.

> MORRIE: It was very interesting how they make one picture into another. I see why they named it *Zoom*. I think they named it that because you zoom out of the picture. It must have been very hard to make this book because they have to think what kind of picture can fit into another.

> SHECARA: I liked reading it backwards because it was like a magnifying glass on a big picture. Rereading it backwards was really fun because you knew what was coming but it was from a different point of view.

Alyssa's written response:

> At the beginning, I thought to myself, 'How can that be?' I turned back a page and realized the letters in the corner. After that, I started to look for hints in the pictures. In the Arizona scene, the third one, I knew it was a stamp because of the edge for example. But I was a little confused at the ending – I thought it was going to go back to the rooster! Another thing I did was imagine what happened after the dot at the end.

And Ethan's written response:

> In the first part of the book I didn't really understand the book to the point that I do now. It was as though the whole world broke down into pieces so that I could look into it. It was as though the whole world froze for

that one glimpse. To the mind it was like an atom bomb going off in my head. And all of a sudden I felt like I should slow down in life and just live life to the fullest because there might be one and only glimpse and that would be just amazing. To me it was like perfectly timed clock work. By far it was the most powerful literature that I have ever read. It was really a philosophical book and it was great.[31]

6.4 Working with senior students

Playful picturebooks have much to offer older readers. In advocating the use of 'postmodern' picturebooks in secondary classrooms, Ken Watson highlights the ways in which the texts reflect 'the cultural and linguistic diversity of our society, [and] provide an economical and eye-and-ear-catching way of investigating the new literacies since meaning is constructed using a variety of semiotic systems.'[32]

There are many ways of encouraging secondary students to engage critically with picturebooks. The comprehensive strategy outlined below covers most of the key issues, does not assume any prior knowledge of picturebook theory, and could be adapted to suit most environments.[33] The strategy entails four basic steps:

- Having an introductory discussion about the author and illustrator, referring to previous works and perhaps considering the definition of 'picturebook', to establish students' prior knowledge.
- Focusing, initially, on the written text which has ideally been copied onto sheets as handouts. (One could, of course, focus on the images first.)
  - Read the text aloud.
  - Discuss central ideas, mood and tone. Can the message be interpreted in several ways? Does reading the text using a different voice influence the interpretation?
  - Identify linguistic features – imagery, emotive language, personification, symbols, exaggeration, puns and sarcasm. Identify setting, characters and genre.
- Asking students to take on the role of illustrator. Each student selects a phrase or paragraph to illustrate in sketch form. Discuss the complexity of the role: literal and implied meanings of the words, page breaks, page layout, color and media.

- Introducing students to the whole book only after steps 1–3.
  - Study the cover. What does it say about intended audience, tone and genre?
  - Examine the illustrations closely. How do they enhance or extend the written text? Do they shape the reader's interpretation of the words?
  - Look at symbols, colors, layout, intertextual references, characterization and the effect of the media used for the pictures.
  - What part does the illustrative text play in the construction of the narrative?
  - Do the pictures help to create multiple readings of the story?

An inclusive approach such as this one helps to build skills and self-confidence. As students become more familiar with narrative structure, visual grammar and literary techniques, they will learn to trust their judgement, confident that they can support their opinions with evidence from the text. Readers will also become more attuned to structural patterns, the interplay of written text and illustrations, and the layers of meaning at work in the text.

Playful multimodal texts can also be an excellent resource for introducing key issues in literary theory to secondary students. John Stephens, Ken Watson and Judith Parker have produced an outstanding teaching resource[34] which includes a number of the texts examined in this book. Working in small groups, students can explore concepts such as the constructedness of texts (*Bear Hunt*), textual gaps (John Burningham's *Granpa*), unreliable narrators/intertextuality (versions of The Three Pigs story), intertextuality/ visual literacy (*The Lost Thing*), focalization (*Voices in the Park*), and metafiction (*Black and White* and *The Three Pigs*). Other critical perspectives discussed in the volume include reader response and reception theories, theories of feminism, post-colonial literary theory, and deconstruction.

Ultimately, however, it would be unwise to treat theoretical knowledge as an end in itself. Textual playfulness is intrinsically valuable. As I have demonstrated, its value lies in its insistence on seeking out other points of view; its support for metalinguistic awareness and reflexive, speculative thinking; and its infinite capacity to surprise and delight.

Notes

1 Ethan is a fifth-grade student who took part in Sylvia Pantaleo's study: '"How could that be?": reading Banyai's *Zoom* and *Re-Zoom*,' *Language Arts* 84(3) (2007), 232.

2 I am indebted to the UK Chartered Institute of Library and Information Professionals (CILIP) Kate Greenaway Visual Literacy project for helping me frame these objectives (and giving me a title for this chapter: 'Learning to look'). Excellent resource material can be found at www.carnegiegreenaway. org.uk/celebration/reading_resources.php#reader_development_pack_2.

3 Visual elements are based on the work of G. Kress and T. van Leeuwen, in *Reading Images: A Grammar of Visual Design* (London: Routledge, 1996), and Michele Anstey, 'Postmodern picturebook as artefact: developing tools for an archaeological dig,' in *Postmodern Picturebooks: Play, Parody and Self-Referentiality*, eds. Lawrence R. Sipe and Sylvia Pantaleo (New York: Routledge, 2008), 147–163. David Lewis's *Reading Contemporary Picturebooks: Picturing Text* (London: Routledge/Falmer, 2001) is another valuable resource which covers all aspects of picturebook design and production.

4 The picture walk is described in detail by Melissa Thibault in 'Reading picture books,' retrieved on 28 June 2014 from www.learnnc.org/lp/pages/669. LEARN NC is a program of the University of North Carolina at Chapel Hill School of Education.

5 Thibault, 'Reading picture books,' 2.

6 Janet C. Richards and Nancy A. Anderson in 'What do I *see*? What do I *think*? What do I *wonder*? (STW): A visual literacy strategy to help emergent readers focus on storybook illustrations,' *The Reading Teacher* 56(3) (2003), 442–444.

7 As described by Frank Serafini in '*Voices in the Park*, voices in the classroom: Readers responding to postmodern picture books,' *Reading Research and Instruction* 44(3) (2005), 51.

8 Aidan Chambers, 'The framework of "tell me" questions,' in *Tell Me (Children, Reading and Talk) with The Reading Environment* (Stroud, UK: Thimble Press, 2011; Portland, ME: Stenhouse Publishers, 2011), 172–182.

9 Ibid., 181.

10 See Geoffrey Williams and David Jack, 'The role of story: learning to read in a special education class,' in *Revaluing Troubled Readers*, Occasional Paper no. 15 (Tucson, AZ: Program in Language and Literacy, University of Arizona, 1986), 12–39. It should be noted that the children in this class could not read prose when they started working with Williams and Jack. As mentioned, their reading education up to that time had focused on rote learning with flash cards and it was evident that they neither understood the meanings of the words

which they struggled to decode nor remembered them from one reading session to the next.

11 Ibid., 21–22.

12 Ibid., 37.

13 Ibid., 26–27.

14 Lewis, *Reading Contemporary Picturebooks*, 60, note 2.

15 Ibid., 56.

16 Ibid., 46, 58.

17 Ibid., 56–57.

18 Ibid., 58.

19 Lawrence R. Sipe, 'First graders interpret David Wiesner's *The Three Pigs*: a case study,' in Sipe and Pantaleo, *Postmodern Picturebooks*, 223–237.

20 Ibid., 225.

21 Ibid., 227–228.

22 Ibid., 229–230.

23 Ibid., 230.

24 Ibid., 235.

25 Serafini, '*Voices in the Park*, voices in the classroom,' 47–64.

26 Ibid., 51.

27 Ibid., 53–54.

28 Ibid., 55.

29 Ibid., 55.

30 Ibid., 58–59.

31 Pantaleo, '"How could that be?",' 222, 227, 228, 232.

32 Ken Watson, 'The postmodern picture book in the secondary classroom,' *English in Australia* 140 (2004), 55.

33 The strategy was developed by Lesley Reece of The Literature Centre, Fremantle, Western Australia.

34 John Stephens, Ken Watson and Judith Parker, *From Picture Book to Literary Theory* (Sydney: St Clair Press, 2003).

Bibliography

Playful texts and playbooks cited in this book

Ahlberg, Allan and Bruce Ingman. *The Pencil*. London: Walker Books, 2008. Somerville, MA: Candlewick Press, 2008.

Ahlberg, Janet and Allan Ahlberg. *Peepo!* 1981. Harmondsworth and New York: Puffin Books, 2011.

Ahlberg, Janet and Allan Ahlberg. *Each Peach Pear Plum*. London: Viking, 1978. Harmondsworth and New York: Puffin Books, 1988.

Ahlberg, Janet and Allan Ahlberg. *The Jolly Pocket Postman*. London: William Heinemann, 1995. New York: Little, Brown and Company, 1995.

Ahlberg, Janet and Allan Ahlberg. *The Worm Book*. Harmondsworth and New York: Puffin Books, 2000.

Andersen, Hans Christian. *The Complete Illustrated Stories of Hans Christian Andersen*. Illustrated by A. W. Baynes. Translated by H. W. Dulcken. London: Chancellor Press, 1983.

Anno, Mitsumasa. *Anno's Peekaboo*. New York: Philomel, 1988.

Anno, Mitsumasa and Masaichiro Anno. *Anno's Magical ABC: An Anamorphic Alphabet*. London: The Bodley Head, 1981. New York: Putnam, 1981.

Anno, Mitsumasa and Tuyosi Mori. *Anno's Three Pigs*. London: The Bodley Head, 1985. Toronto: Random House of Canada, 1986.

Baillie, Allan and Jane Tanner. *Drac and the Gremlin*. Ringwood, Australia: Viking Kestrel, 1988. New York: Puffin Books, 1992.

Banks, Lynne Reid. *The Indian in the Cupboard*. London: J. M. Dent and Sons, 1981. London: Collins, 1995. New York: Yearling, 2010.

Banyai, Istvan. *Zoom*. New York: Viking, 1995. Harmondsworth and New York: Puffin Books, 1995.

Base, Graeme. *The Eleventh Hour*. Ringwood, Australia: Viking Kestrel, 1988. Harmondsworth and New York: Puffin Books, 1997.

Bourke, Linda. *Eye Spy*. San Francisco, CA: Chronicle Books, 1991.

Brown, Margaret Wise and Clement Hurd. *Goodnight Moon*. 1947. New York: HarperCollins, 2006. London: Macmillan, 2010.

Browne, Anthony. *A Walk in the Park*. London: Julia MacRae, 1977. New York: Macmillan Children's Books, 1977.

Browne, Anthony. *Bear Hunt*. London: Hamish Hamilton, 1979. Harmondsworth and New York: Puffin Books, 1994.

Browne, Anthony. *Through the Magic Mirror*. New York: Greenwillow Books, 1992. London: Walker Books, 2010.

Browne, Anthony. *Voices in the Park*. London: Doubleday, 1998. New York: Dorling Kindersley Children, 2001.

Burningham, John. *Come Away from the Water, Shirley*. London: Jonathan Cape, 1977. Red Fox Books, 1992.

Burningham, John. *Time to Get Out of the Bath, Shirley*. London: Jonathan Cape, 1978. Red Fox Books, 1994.

Busch, Wilhelm. *Max and Moritz*. 1865. Translated and edited by H. Arthur Klein. New York: Dover Publications, 1962.

Carroll, Lewis. *Alice's Adventures in Wonderland*. 1865. Available at www. gutenberg.org/files/11/11-h/11-h.htm.

Carroll, Lewis. *Through the Looking Glass and What Alice Found There*. 1871. Available at www.gutenberg.org/files/12/12-h/12-h.htm.

Carter, David A. *One Red Dot*. New York: Little Simon, 2005.

Carter, David A. *600 Black Spots*. New York: Little Simon, 2007.

Chambers, Aidan. *Breaktime*. London: The Bodley Head, 1978. Reissued (with *Dance on My Grave*) by Random House as a Definitions paperback, 2007.

Child, Lauren. *I Will Not Ever Never Eat a Tomato*. London: Orchard Books, 2000. Somerville, MA: Candlewick Press, 2003.

Child, Lauren. *Who's Afraid of the Big Bad Book*. London: Hodder Children's Books, 2002. New York: Disney-Hyperion, 2003.

Child, Lauren. *Ruby Redfort: Look Into My Eyes*. London: HarperCollins, 2011. Somerville, MA: Candlewick Press, 2012.

Child, Lauren. *Ruby Redfort: Take Your Last Breath*. London: HarperCollins, 2012. Somerville, MA: Candlewick Press, 2013.

Child, Lauren. *Ruby Redfort: Catch Your Death*. London: HarperCollins, 2013.

Clements, Andrew. *Frindle*. Illustrated by Brian Selznick. New York: Atheneum Books, 1998.

Collodi, Carlo. *Pinocchio*. 1883. Illustrated by Gioia Fiammenghi. Translated by E. Harden. Harmondsworth: Puffin Books, 1974. Illustrated by Fulvio Testa. Translated by Geoffrey Brock. New York: The New York Review Children's Collection, 2012.

Dahl, Roald. *Revolting Rhymes*. Illustrated by Quentin Blake. Harmondsworth and New York: Puffin Books, 1984.

Donaldson, Julia and Axel Scheffler. *Charlie Cook's Favourite Book*. London: Macmillan Children's Books, 2005. New York: Dial, 2006.

Faller, Régis. *Polo: The Runaway Book*. New Milford, CT: Roaring Brook Press, 2007.

French, Jackie. *The Shaggy Gully Times*. Illustrated by Bruce Whatley. Sydney: Angus and Robertson, 2007.

Gaiman, Neil. *Coraline*. London: Bloomsbury, 2002. New York: William Morrow Paperbacks, 2006.

Godden, Rumer. *The Doll's House*. 1947. London: Macmillan Children's Books, 2006.

Gravett, Emily. *The Rabbit Problem*. London: Macmillan Children's Books, 2009. New York: Simon and Schuster, 2010 (pop-up edition).

Gravett, Emily. *Wolves*. London: Macmillan Children's Books, 2005. New York: Simon and Schuster, 2006.

Hall, Michael. *My Heart Is Like a Zoo*. New York: Greenwillow Books, 2010.

Handford, Martin. *Where's Wally?* London: Walker Books, 1987. In the U.S. and Canada published as *Where's Waldo?* Somerville, MA: Candlewick Press, 1987.

Hoban, Russell. *The Mouse and His Child*. 1967. Illustrated by Lillian Hoban. London: Faber and Faber, 2000. Illustrated by David Small. New York: Arthur A. Levine Books, 2001.

Hoban, Russell. *La Corona and the Tin Frog*. Illustrated by Nicola Bayley. London: Jonathan Cape, 1979. New York: Smithmark Publishers, 1987.

Hoban, Russell and Colin McNaughton. *The Flight of Bembel Rudzuk*. London: Methuen/Walker, 1982. New York: Philomel, 1982.

Hoffmann, E. T. A. 'The Sandman' and 'Nutcracker and the King of Mice' (1816) in *The Best Tales of Hoffmann*. Edited by E. F. Bleiler. New York: Dover Publications, 1967.

Holub, Joan. *Little Red Writing*. Illustrated by Melissa Sweet. San Francisco, CA: Chronicle Books, 2013.

Hutchins, Pat. *Rosie's Walk*. London: The Bodley Head, 1968. New York: Simon and Schuster, 1968.

Jansson, Tove. *The Book about Moomin, Mymble and Little My*. Helsinki: Holger Schildts Förlag, 1952. English translation by Sophie Hannah. London: Sort of Books, 2001.

Johnson, Crockett. *Harold and the Purple Crayon*. 1955. New York: HarperCollins, 1998.

Joyce, William. *The Fantastic Flying Books of Mr. Morris Lessmore*. Illustrated by William Joyce and Joe Bluhm. New York: Atheneum Books for Young Readers, 2012.

Juster, Norton. *The Phantom Tollbooth.* Illustrated by Jules Feiffer. London: Collins, 1974. New York: Yearling, 1996.

Lear, Edward. *The Adventures of Mr Lear, the Polly and the Pusseybite on Their Way to the Ritertitle Mountains.* Private correspondence. August 23, 1866. Available at www.nonsenselit.org/Lear/pw/riter.html.

Lear, Edward. 'Manypeeplia upsidownia' from *Nonsense Songs.* 1894. Retrieved on 28 June 2014 from www.gutenberg.org/files/13647/13647-h/13647-h.htm#botany.

Lear, Edward. 'Piggiwiggia pyramidalis' from *Nonsense Songs.* 1894. Retrieved on 28 June 2014 from www.gutenberg.org/files/13647/13647-h/13647-h.htm#botany.

Legge, David. *Bamboozled.* Sydney: Scholastic, 1994. New York: Scholastic, 1995.

Lehman, Barbara. *The Red Book.* Boston, MA: Houghton Mifflin, 2004.

Macaulay, David. *Black and White.* Boston, MA: Houghton Mifflin, 1990. London: Hodder and Stoughton, 1990.

Martin, Bill, Jr. and John Archambault. *Chicka Chicka Boom Boom.* Illustrated by Lois Ehlert. New York: Simon and Schuster, 1989.

Masefield, John. *The Midnight Folk.* London: William Heinemann, 1927. New York: The New York Review Children's Collection, 2008.

McCaughrean, Geraldine. *A Pack of Lies: Twelve Stories in One.* Oxford: Oxford University Press, 1988. New York: Scholastic, 1991.

McCay, Winsor. *Little Nemo in Slumberland.* 1904-1914. Available at http://comicstriplibrary.org/browse/results?title=2.

McNaughton, Colin. *Suddenly!* London: Andersen Press, 1994.

McNaughton, Colin. *Boo!* London: Andersen Press, 1995.

McNaughton, Colin. *Oops!* London: Andersen Press, 1996.

McNaughton, Colin. *Oomph!* London: Andersen Press, 2001.

Milne, A. A. *Winnie-the-Pooh.* Illustrated by Ernest Shepherd. 1926. London: Methuen, 2001. New York: Dutton Juvenile, 2001.

Nesbit, E. *The Story of the Treasure Seekers.* 1899. Harmondsworth: Puffin Books, 1996. San Francisco, CA: Chronicle Books, 2006.

Pieńkowski, Jan. *Haunted House.* London: Heinemann, 1979.

Pieńkowski, Jan. *Robot.* London: Heinemann, 1981.

Portis, Antoinette. *Not a Stick.* New York: HarperCollins, 2008.

Pratchett, Terry. *The Amazing Maurice and His Educated Rodents.* Illustrated by David Wyatt. London: Corgi Books, 2002. New York: HarperCollins, 2008.

Pullman, Philip. *Clockwork or All Wound Up.* Illustrated by Peter Bailey. London: Corgi Yearling Books, 1996. Illustrated by Leonid Gore. New York: Scholastic, 1998. Illustrated by Kevin Hawkes. New York: Yearling Books, 2002.

Pullman, Philip. *I Was a Rat! … or The Scarlet Slippers.* Illustrated by Peter Bailey. London: Corgi Yearling Books, 2000. Illustrated by Kevin Hawkes. New York: Knopf, 2000.

Ransome, Arthur. *Swallows and Amazons.* 1930. London: Red Fox, 2010. Boston, MA: David R. Godine Publisher, 2013.

Rosenthal, Amy Krouse and Tom Lichtenheld. *Duck! Rabbit!* San Francisco, CA: Chronicle Books, 2009.

Scieszka, Jon and Daniel Adel. *The Book That Jack Wrote.* New York: Viking, 1994.

Scieszka, Jon and Lane Smith. *The True Story of the Three Little Pigs.* New York: Viking, 1989.

Scieszka, Jon and Lane Smith. *The Stinky Cheese Man and Other Fairly Stupid Tales.* New York: Viking, 1992.

Scieszka, Jon and Lane Smith. *Squids Will Be Squids: Fresh Morals, Beastly Tales.* New York: Viking, 1998.

Scieszka, Jon and Lane Smith. *Baloney (Henry P.).* New York: Viking, 2001.

Seidmann-Freud, Tom. *The Magic Boat: A Book to Turn and Move.* 1929. Los Angeles, CA: Ernest Benn, 1981.

Seuss, Dr. *On Beyond Zebra.* 1955. New York: Random House, 2003. London: HarperCollins, 2004.

Seuss, Dr. *The Cat in the Hat.* 1957. New York: Random House, 2014. London: HarperCollins, 2011.

Seuss, Dr. *The Cat in the Hat Comes Back.* 1958. New York: Random House, 2012. London: HarperCollins, 2011.

Seuss, Dr. *Dr. Seuss's ABC.* 1963. New York: Random House, 2014. London: HarperCollins, 2003.

Sidman, Joyce. *Meow Ruff.* Illustrated by Michelle Berg. Boston, MA: Houghton Mifflin, 2006.

Smith, Lane. *It's a Book.* New York: Roaring Brook Press, 2010. London: Macmillan Children's Books, 2012.

Spiegelman, Art. *Open Me ... I'm a Dog!* New York: Joanna Cutler Books, 1997.

Tan, Shaun. *The Lost Thing.* Sydney: Lothian, 2000. New York: Arthur A. Levine Books, 2007.

Tenniel, John. Illustrations from *Alice's Adventures in Wonderland* and *Through the Looking-Glass and What Alice Found There.* Retrieved on 28 June 2014 from www.alice-in-wonderland.net/alice2b.html.

Trivizas, Eugene and Helen Oxenbury, *The Three Little Wolves and the Big Bad Pig.* London: Egmont, 1993. New York: Margaret K. McElderry Books, 1997.

Van Allsburg, Chris. *The Mysteries of Harris Burdick.* Boston, MA: Houghton Mifflin, 1984. London: Andersen Press, 1984.

Watt, Mélanie. *Chester.* Toronto: Kids Can Press, 2009.

Wiesner, David. *The Three Pigs.* New York: Clarion Books, 2001. London: Andersen Press, 2012.

Wiesner, David. *Flotsam.* New York: Clarion Books, 2006. London: Andersen Press, 2012.

Wiesner, David. *Mr Wuffles!* New York: Clarion Books, 2013. London: Andersen Press, 2013.

Wilbur, Richard. *The Disappearing Alphabet.* Illustrated by David Diaz. San Diego, CA: Harcourt Brace and Company, 1998.

Williams, Margery. *The Velveteen Rabbit.* Illustrated by William Nicholson. 1922. New York: Doubleday Books for Young Readers, 2014.

Further reading: more playful texts

Ahlberg, Allan and Bruce Ingman. *The Runaway Dinner.* London: Walker Books, 2006. Somerville, MA: Candlewick Press, 2006. Companion to *The Pencil.* A hungry boy gives chase when his sausage makes a run for it.

Ahlberg, Allan and Bruce Ingman. *Previously.* London: Walker Books, 2007. Somerville, MA: Candlewick Press, 2007. Nursery rhymes unfold in reverse order. Challenging, witty and engaging.

Ahlberg, Janet and Allan Ahlberg. *The Jolly Postman or Other People's Letters.* London: William Heinemann, 1986. New York: Little, Brown and Company, 1986. Acclaimed interactive picturebook containing miniature letters and cards for fairytale characters. Reprinted many times.

Allen, Pamela. *Bertie.* Ringwood, Australia: Puffin Books, 2013. A reversible text which examines the effects our emotions have on others.

Bachelet, Gilles. *My Cat, the Silliest Cat in the World.* Translated by Nicholas Elliot. New York: Abrams Books, 2006. Words and images contradict each other. The narrator is strangely unaware that his cat is actually an elephant. Also see *When the Silliest Cat Was Small* (2007).

Briggs, Raymond. *The Puddleman.* London: Jonathan Cape, 2004. In its re-enactment of symbolic play, *The Puddleman* incorporates different kinds of language play, particularly play with nominalization.

Brown, Ruth. *A Dark, Dark Tale.* Harmondsworth: Puffin Books, 1992. A retelling of a traditional rhyme. Play with patterns of accumulation and embedding. Captivating illustrations.

Browne, Anthony. *Gorilla.* London and Boston, MA: Walker Books, 1983. A metafictive take on the theme of toys coming to life. Profoundly intertextual.

Browne, Anthony. *Willy the Dreamer.* London and Boston, MA: Walker Books, 1997. An intertextual celebration of Surrealism, children's literature and popular culture.

Browne, Anthony. *My Dad.* London: Doubleday Children's Books, 2000. New York: Farrar, Straus and Giroux, 2001. Extended play with figurative language and visual nonsense. Also see companion titles *My Mum/My Mom*, and *My Brother*.

Carle, Eric. *The Very Hungry Caterpillar*. New York: Putnam, 1969. London: Hamish Hamilton, 1969. Reprinted in 2003. The classic story about the metamorphosis of a butterfly. Simple die-cuts and vibrant collage. Wonderful use of lists.

Carter, David A. *How Many Bugs in a Box?* New York: Little Simon, 2006. Acclaimed pop-up counting book. Clever paper engineering and playful narrative.

Child, Lauren. *Utterly Me, Clarice Bean*. London: Orchard Books, 2002. Somerville, MA: Candlewick Press, 2005. The first in the series of Clarice Bean novels. Metafictive wit and dry humor.

Child, Lauren. *Slightly Invisible*. London: Orchard Books, 2010. Somerville, MA: Candlewick Press, 2011. Another in the Charlie and Lola series of picturebooks. All titles are recommended.

Cottin, Menena and Rosana Faría. *The Black Book of Colors*. Toronto: Groundwood Books, 2008. Tactile play with simile and metaphor. Remarkable black-on-black illustrations accompanied by Braille text.

Curtis, Neil and Joan Grant. *Cat and Fish*. South Melbourne: Lothian Books, 2003. A nonsense tale about the coexistence of opposites. Exquisite black-and-white engravings and innovative design.

Curtis, Neil and Joan Grant. *Cat and Fish Go to See*. South Melbourne: Lothian Books, 2005. Even more audacious in design. Extensive wordplay and optical illusions.

Donaldson, Julia and Axel Scheffler. *Tiddler*. London: Alison Green Books, 2008. New York: Arthur A. Levine Books, 2008. Wordplay and offbeat rhythms in this celebration of storytelling.

Donaldson, Julia and Axel Scheffler. *Stick Man*. London: Alison Green Books, 2009. New York: Arthur A. Levine Books, 2009. Lively rhyming text with intertextual allusions.

Donaldson, Julia and David Roberts. *Jack and the Flumflum Tree*. London: Macmillan Children's Books, 2011. New York: Arthur A. Levine Books, 2013. Learesque nonsense verse.

Fanelli, Sarah. *The Onion's Great Escape*. London: Phaidon Press, 2012. New York: Phaidon Press, 2012. A multilayered, interrogative text which is transformed (into an onion) in the reading process. Outstanding design.

Fardell, John. *The Day Louis Got Eaten*. London and New York: Andersen Press, 2012. Cumulative nonsense. Witty and inventive.

Foley, James. *In the Lion*. Sydney: Walker Books, 2012. A chain verse with striking illustrations.

Freedman, Deborah. *Scribble*. New York: Knopf Books for Young Readers, 2007. Metaleptic playfulness. A squiggle takes on a life of its own in this story of two sisters and their scribbling rivalry.

Ga'g, Wanda and Howard Ga'g. 1933. *The ABC Bunny*. Minneapolis, MN: University of Minnesota Press, 2004. An outstanding alphabet book with full musical score and beautiful lithographs.

Gaiman, Neil and Charles Vess. *Instructions*. London: Bloomsbury, 2010. New York: HarperCollins, 2010. Playful metafiction. Maxims for fairytale travelers.

Graham, Bob. *Dimity Dumpty: The Story of Humpty's Little Sister*. Somerville, MA: Candlewick Press, 2007. Newtown, Australia: Walker Books, 2009. Warm, intertextual humor.

Gravett, Emily. *Again!* London: Macmillan Children's Books, 2012. New York: Simon and Schuster, 2013. More metafictive play with narrative conventions. Cedric the dragon jumps in and out of the story, and burns his way through the book.

Hall, Michael. *Cat Tale*. New York: Greenwillow Books, 2012. A witty tongue-twister told in homonyms. Verbal and visual nonsense.

Hoban, Russell and Colin McNaughton. *They Came from Aargh!* London: Methuen, 1981. New York: Philomel, 1981. Exuberant wordplay. Also see the other books in 'The Hungry Three' series: *The Great Fruit Gum Robbery* (1981), *The Flight of Bembel Rudzuk* (1982), and *The Battle of Zormla* (1982).

Horáček, Petr. *Jonathan and Martha*. London: Phaidon Press, 2012. New York: Phaidon Press, 2012. Vibrant collage and ingenious die-cuts. Play with the fabric of the book and an engaging narrative about coexistence.

Howitt, Mary and Tony Di Terlizzi. *The Spider and the Fly*. New York: Simon and Schuster, 2002. *The Spider and the Fly* is based on Mary Howitt's poem, first published in 1829 and parodied by Lewis Carroll in 'The Lobster Quadrille'. This intertextual version features Gothic illustrations, an afterword by the spider, and an appeal to Charlotte (heroine of *Charlotte's Web*).

Jeffers, Oliver. *The Incredible Book Eating Boy*. New York: Philomel, 2007. Meta-linguistic and bibliophilic!

Johnson, D. B. *Palazzo Inverso*. Boston, MA: Houghton Mifflin, 2010. Visual nonsense. This homage to Escher invites readers into a topsy-turvy world which makes sense forwards, backwards, and upside down. Flip each double page spread for a discrete story within the story.

Klassen, Jon. *I Want My Hat Back*. London: Walker Books, 2011. Somerville, MA: Candlewick Press, 2011. Play with inferred meanings and gaps in the text. Also see *This Is Not My Hat* (2012).

Lehman, Barbara. *Museum Trip*. Boston, MA: Houghton Mifflin, 2006. A wordless picturebook. Intriguing embedded stories.

Lester, Alison. *Imagine*. Crows Nest, Australia: Allen and Unwin, 1989. Boston, MA: Houghton Mifflin, 1990. *Imagine* combines make-believe play with meticulous cataloguing of the natural world.

MacRae, Tom and Elena Odriozola. *The Opposite*. Atlanta, GA: Peachtree Publishers, 2006. London: Andersen Press, 2007. Imaginative play with ontological concepts.

McKee, David. *Not Now, Bernard*. London: Andersen Press, 1980. Reprinted, 2012. Bernard is consumed by a purple monster while his parents attend to other matters.

McNaughton, Colin and Emma Chichester Clark. *Have You Ever Ever Ever?* London: Walker Books, 2011. A playful homage to Mother Goose.

Messenger, Norman. *Imagine*. Somerville, MA: Candlewick Press, 2005. Moving parts and challenging optical illusions. Intertextual play with speculative thinking.

Quay, Emma. *Not a Cloud in the Sky*. Sydney: HarperCollins, 2013. Exploration of perspective taking in symbolic play.

Sendak, Maurice. *In the Night Kitchen*. New York: Harper and Row, 1970. New York: HarperCollins, 1996. London: Red Fox Books, 2001. Rich intertextuality. Sendak has acknowledged the particular influence of Winsor McCay's *Little Nemo* comic strips. Sendak's masterpiece, *Where the Wild Things Are*, celebrates play but is not, strictly speaking, a playful text in the sense that I use the term in this book.

Snell, Gordon and David McKee. *The King of Quizzical Island*. Somerville, MA: Candlewick Press, 2009. A curious king sets sail for the edge of the world. Nonsense verse in the tradition of Seuss, Juster and Lear.

Staake, Bob. *Look! A Book!* New York: Little, Brown and Company, 2011. An exuberant 'I spy' book with die-cuts on every page revealing surprising connections between disparate objects. Also see its companion, *Look! Another Book!* (2012).

Swanson, Susan Marie and Beth Krommes. *The House in the Night*. Boston, MA: Houghton Mifflin Harcourt, 2011 (board book edition). A cumulative story with intertextual elements and radiant black, white and gold illustrations.

Tullet, Hervé. *The Game of Shadows*. London: Phaidon Press, 2013 (board book edition). A die-cut board book featuring black-on-black illustrations. Imaginative play with visual metaphor. Best read in the dark with a torch to bring the stories to life. This is one of a series of playful board book games by Tullet.

Van Allsburg, Chris. *Bad Day at Riverbend*. Boston, MA: HMH Books for Young Readers, 1995. In this living coloring-in book, the black-and-white town and townspeople of Riverbend are infested by looping squiggles and waxy stripes of color. Inspired by Harold and his purple crayon.

Vere, Ed. *The Getaway*. New York: Margaret K. McElderrry Books, 2006. A self-reflexive heist story with embedded text (*The Getaway Movie* starring Roman Ratanski).

Vipont, Elfrida and Raymond Briggs. *The Elephant and the Bad Baby*. Harmondsworth: Puffin Books, 1971. New York: Putnam, 2000. Harmondsworth: Puffin Books, 2007. A joyful chain verse.

Wiesner, David. *Tuesday*. New York: Clarion Books, 1991. Features a mysterious night flight by a squadron of flying frogs. Play with perspective, proportion and probability.

Yaccarino, Dan. *Good Night, Mr Night*. Boston, MA: Houghton Mifflin Harcourt, 2004. A picturebook lullaby. Imaginative play with metaphor.

Other works cited

Anstey, Michele. "'It's not all black and white": postmodern picture books and new literacies.' *Journal of Adolescent and Adult Literacy*, 45(6) (2002), 444–458.

Anstey, Michele. 'Postmodern picturebook as artefact: developing tools for an archaeological dig.' In *Postmodern Picturebooks: Play, Parody and Self-Referentiality*. Edited by Lawrence R. Sipe and Sylvia Pantaleo, 147–163. New York: Routledge, 2008.

Anstey, Michele and Geoff Bull. 'Helping teachers explore multimodal texts.' *Curriculum Leadership* (now *Curriculum and Leadership Journal*) 8(16) (2010). Retrieved on 28 June 2014 from www.curriculum.edu.au/leader/helping_teachers_to_explore_multimodal_texts,31522.html?issueID=12207.

Appleyard, J. A. *Becoming a Reader: The Experience of Fiction from Childhood to Adulthood*. New York: Cambridge University Press, 1994.

Bakhtin, M. M. *The Dialogic Imagination: Four Essays*. Edited by Michael Holquist. Translated by Caryl Emerson and Michael Holquist. Austin: University of Texas Press, 1981.

Baron-Cohen, Simon. 'Theory of mind in normal development and autism.' *Prisme* 34 (2001), 174–183. Retrieved on 28 June 2014 from www.autism-community.com/wp-content/uploads/2010/11/TOM-in-TD-and-ASD.pdf.

Barthes, Roland. *Image, Music, Text*. Translated by Stephen Heath. New York: The Noonday Press, 1977.

Bateson, Gregory. 'The message "this is play".' In *Child's Play*. Edited by R. E. Herron and Brian Sutton-Smith, 261–266. New York: John Wiley and Sons, 1971.

Bateson, Gregory. *Steps to an Ecology of Mind: Collected Essays in Anthropology, Psychiatry, Evolution and Epistemology*. Chicago, IL: University of Chicago Press, 2000.

Bergen, Doris. 'The role of pretend play in children's cognitive development.' In the *Journal of Early Childhood Research and Practice* 4(1) (2002). Retrieved on 28 June 2014 from http://ecrp.uiuc.edu/v4n1/bergen.html.

Bretherton, Inge. 'Representing the social world in symbolic play: reality and fantasy.' In *Symbolic Play: The Development of Social Understanding*. Edited by Inge Bretherton, 3–41. Orlando: Academic Press, 1984.

Bruner, Jerome S. *Child's Talk: Learning to Use Language*. New York: W.W. Norton and Co., 1983.

Bruner, Jerome S. 'Vygotsky: a historical and conceptual perspective.' In *Culture, Communication and Cognition: Vygotskian Perspectives*. Edited by James V. Wertsch, 21–34. Cambridge: Cambridge University Press, 1985.

Bruner, Jerome S. *Actual Minds, Possible Worlds*. Cambridge, MA: Harvard University Press, 1986.

Bruner, Jerome S. and V. Sherwood. 'Peekaboo and the learning of rule structures.' In *Play – Its Role in Development and Evolution*. Edited by Jerome S. Bruner, Alison Jolly and Kathy Sylva, 277–285. Harmondsworth: Penguin Books, 1976.

Caillois, Roger. *Man, Play and Games*. Translated by Meyer Barash. New York: Free Press of Glencoe, 1961.

Carey, Joanna. 'Bruce Ingman: the line of beauty', *The Guardian*, Saturday 20 June 2009. Retrieved on 28 June 2014 from www.guardian.co.uk/books/2009/jun/20/bruce-ingham. (This is the correct URL despite the misspelling of 'Ingman' at the end.)

Cazden, Courtney B. 'Play with language and meta-linguistic awareness: one dimension of language experience.' In *Play – Its Role in Development and Evolution*. Edited by Jerome S. Bruner, Alison Jolly and Kathy Sylva, 603–608. Harmondsworth: Penguin Books, 1976.

Cazden, Courtney B. 'Peekaboo as an instructional model: discourse development at home and at school.' In *The Sociogenesis of Language and Human Contact*. Edited by Bruce Bain, 40–42. New York: Plenum Press, 1983.

Chambers, Aidan. 'The reader in the book.' In *Booktalk: Occasional Writing on Literature and Children*, 34–58. London: The Bodley Head, 1985, and Woodchester: The Thimble Press, 1995.

Chambers, Aidan. 'Ways of telling: from writer to reader: an author reads himself.' In *Booktalk*, 92–115.

Chambers, Aidan. 'The framework of "Tell me" questions.' In *Tell Me (Children, Reading and Talk) with The Reading Environment*, 172–182. Woodchester: The Thimble Press, 2011; Portland, ME: Stenhouse Publishers, 2011.

Chukovsky, Kornei. *From Two to Five*. Translated and edited by Miriam Morton. Berkeley, CA: University of California Press, 1963.

Clark, Katerina and Michael Holquist. *Mikhail Bakhtin*. Cambridge, MA: Harvard University Press, 1984.

Cohen, David. *The Development of Play*, 2nd ed. London: Routledge, 1993.

Cohen, Shlomith. 'Connecting through riddles, or the riddle of connecting.' In *Untying the Knot: On Riddles and Other Enigmatic Modes*. Edited by Galit

Hasan-Rokem and David Shulman, 294–315. New York: Oxford University Press, 1996.

Cook, Guy. *Language Play, Language Learning.* Oxford: Oxford University Press, 2000.

Crystal, David. *Language Play.* Harmondsworth: Penguin Books, 1998.

Dällenbach, Lucien. *The Mirror in the Text.* Translated by Jeremy Whiteley with Emma Hughes. Cambridge: Polity Press, 1989.

Douglas, Mary. 'Jokes.' In *Implicit Meanings: Essays in Anthropology.* London: Routledge and Keegan Paul, 1975.

Ede, Lisa S. 'An introduction to the nonsense literature of Edward Lear and Lewis Carroll.' In *Explorations in the Field of Nonsense.* Edited by Wim Tigges, 47–60. Amsterdam: Rodopi, 1987.

Fein, Greta. 'The self-building potential of pretend play or "I got a fish, all by myself".' In *Child's Play: Developmental and Applied.* Edited by Thomas D. Yawkey and Anthony D. Pellegrini, 125–141. Hillsdale, NJ: Lawrence Erlbaum Associates, 1984.

Flavell, J. H. 'The development of children's knowledge about the mind: from cognitive connections to mental representations.' In *Developing Theories of Mind.* Edited by J. W. Astington, P. L. Harris, and D. R. Olson, 244–267. New York: Cambridge University Press, 1988.

Friends of the Saint Paul Public Library. 'A conversation with Michael Hall.' Retrieved on 28 June 2014 from www.thefriends.org/wp-content/uploads/2012/12/my-heart-is-like-a-zoo.pdf.

Freud, Sigmund. 'The uncanny.' In *Art and Literature.* Edited by Albert Dickson. Translated by James Strachey. The Penguin Freud Library vol. 14, 339–376. Harmondsworth: Penguin Books, 1990.

Gardner, Martin. Notes to *The Annotated Alice: The Definitive Edition.* Harmondsworth: Penguin Books, 2000. New York: W. W. Norton, 2000.

Garvey, Catherine. *Play,* revised ed. Cambridge, MA: Harvard University Press, 1990.

Genette, Gérard. 'Voice.' In *Narratology: An Introduction.* Edited by Susan Onega and José Ángel Garcia Landa, 173–189. London: Longman, 1996.

Giffin, Holly. 'The coordination of meaning in the creation of a shared make-believe reality.' In *Symbolic Play: The Development of Social Understanding.* Edited by Inge Bretherton, 73–100. Orlando: Academic Press, 1984.

Goldman, L. R. *Child's Play: Myth, Mimesis and Make-Believe.* Oxford: Berg, 1998.

Goldstone, Bette. 'The paradox of space in postmodern picturebooks.' In *Postmodern Picturebooks: Play, Parody and Self-Referentiality.* Edited by Lawrence R. Sipe and Sylvia Pantaleo, 117–129. New York: Routledge, 2008.

Guttman, Marilyn and Carl H. Frederiksen. 'Preschool children's narratives: linking story comprehension, production and play discourse.' In *Play, Language and Stories: The Development of Children's Literate Behaviour*. Edited by Lee Galda and Anthony D. Pelligrini, 99–128. Norwood, NJ: Ablex Publishing Corp, 1985.

Halliday, M. A. K. and Christian Matthiessen. *Construing Experience Through Meaning: A Language Based Approach to Cognition*. London: Cassell, 1999.

Handelman, Don. 'Traps of trans-formation: theoretical convergences between riddle and ritual.' In *Untying the Knot: On Riddles and Other Enigmatic Modes*. Edited by Galit Hasan-Rokem and David Shulman, 37–61. New York: Oxford University Press, 1996.

Hasan-Rokem, Galit and David Shulman. 'Introduction.' In *Untying the Knot: On Riddles and Other Enigmatic Modes*. Edited by Galit Hasan-Rokem and David Shulman, 3–9. New York: Oxford University Press, 1996.

Hobson, Peter R. 'Perceiving attitudes, conceiving minds.' In *Children's Early Understanding of Mind: Origins and Development*. Edited by Charlie Lewis and Peter Mitchell, 71–93. Hove: Lawrence Erlbaum, 1994.

Holmes, Linda A. 'Language play as response discourse.' *Language Arts* 76(3) (1999), 258–262.

Huizinga, Johan. *Homo Ludens: A Study of the Play Element in Culture*. Boston, MA: Beacon Press, 1955.

Iser, Wolfgang. *The Act of Reading: A Theory of Aesthetic Response*. Baltimore, MD: Johns Hopkins University Press, 1978.

Iser, Wolfgang. 'The reading process: a phenomenological approach.' In *Reader Response Criticism: From Formalism to Post-Structuralism*. Edited by Jane P. Tompkins, 50–69. Baltimore, MD: Johns Hopkins University Press, 1980.

Iser, Wolfgang. *The Fictive and the Imaginary: Charting Literary Anthropology*. Baltimore: Johns Hopkins University Press, 1993.

Jones, Dudley. 'Only make-believe? Lies, fictions, and metafictions in Geraldine McCaughrean's *A Pack of Lies* and Philip Pullman's *Clockwork*.' *The Lion and the Unicorn* 23(1) (1999), 86–96.

Kavanaugh, Robert D. 'Origins and consequences of social pretend play.' In *The Oxford Handbook of the Development of Play*. Edited by Anthony D. Pellegrini, 296–307. New York: Oxford University Press, 2011.

Kirshenblatt-Gimblett, Barbara. 'Speech play and verbal art.' In *Play and Learning*. Edited by Brian Sutton-Smith, 219–238. New York: Gardner Press, 1979.

Kirshenblatt-Gimblett, Barbara and Joel Sherzer. 'Introduction to speech play.' In *Speech Play: Research and Resources for Studying Linguistic Creativity*. Edited by Barbara Kirshenblatt-Gimblett, 1–16. Philadelphia: University of Pennsylvania Press, 1976.

Kress, G. *Literacy in the New Media Age*. London: Routledge, 2003.

Kress, G. and T. van Leeuwen. *Reading Images: A Grammar of Visual Design*. London: Routledge, 1996.

Kress, G. and T. van Leeuwen. *Multimodal Discourse*. London: Arnold, 2001.

Kristeva, Julia. 'Word, dialogue and novel.' In *The Kristeva Reader*. Edited by Toril Moi, 34–61. Oxford: Blackwell, 1993.

Kuznets, Lois Rostow. *When Toys Come Alive: Narratives of Animation, Metamorphosis and Development*. New Haven: Yale University Press, 1994.

Langdon, John. *Wordplay: The Philosophy, Art, and Science of Ambigrams*. New York: Harcourt Brace Jovanovich, 1992.

Lecercle, Jean-Jacques. *Philosophy of Nonsense: The Intuitions of Victorian Nonsense literature*. London: Routledge, 1994.

Leslie, Alan M. 'Children's understanding of the mental world.' In *The Oxford Companion to the Mind*. Edited by Richard L. Gregory, 139–142. Oxford: Oxford University Press, 1987.

Lewis, David. *Reading Contemporary Picturebooks: Picturing Text*. London: Routledge/Falmer, 2001.

Lewis, David. 'The constructedness of texts: picture books and the metafictive.' *Signal* 62 (1990), 131–146.

Lillard, Angeline S. 'Pretend play skills and the child's theory of mind.' In *Child Development* 64 (1993), 348–371.

Lillard, Angeline S. 'Mother–child fantasy play.' In *The Oxford Handbook of the Development of Play*. Edited by Anthony D. Pellegrini, 284–295. New York: Oxford University Press, 2011.

McCallum, Robyn. 'Very advanced texts: metafictions and experimental work.' In *Understanding Children's Literature: Key essays from the International Encyclopedia of Children's Literature*. Edited by Peter Hunt, 138–150. London: Routledge, 1999.

McCallum, Robyn. 'Would I lie to you? Metalepsis and modal disruption in some "true" fairy tales.' In *Postmodern Picturebooks: Play, Parody and Self-Referentiality*. Edited by Lawrence R. Sipe and Sylvia Pantaleo, 180–192. New York: Routledge, 2008.

McGillis, Roderick. *The Nimble Reader: Literary Theory and Children's Literature*. New York: Twayne Publishers, 1996.

Meek, Margaret. *How Texts Teach What Readers Learn*. Woodchester: The Thimble Press, 1988.

Meek, Margaret. 'Children reading – now.' In *After Alice: Exploring Children's Literature*. Edited by Morag Styles, Eve Bearne and Victor Watson, 172–188. London: Cassell, 1992.

Nel, Philip. *The Annotated Cat: Under the Hats of Seuss and His Cats*. New York: Random House, 2007.

Nel, Philip. *Metafiction for Children*. Video presentation retrieved on 28 June 2014 from www.philnel.com/2010/09/04/more-metafiction.

Ninio, Anat and Jerome Bruner. 'The achievement and antecedents of labelling.' *Journal of Child Language* 5(1) (1978), 1–15.

Nodelman, Perry. *The Pleasures of Children's Literature.* New York: Longman, 1992.

Onega, Susana and José Ángel García Landa. *Narratology: An Introduction.* London: Longman, 1996.

Opie, Iona. *The People in the Playground.* Oxford: Oxford University Press, 1993.

Opie, Iona and Peter Opie. *The Lore and Language of Schoolchildren.* 1959. New York: New York Review Books Classics, 2001.

Pantaleo, Sylvia. '"How could that be?": reading Banyai's *Zoom* and *Re-Zoom*,' *Language Arts* 84(3) (2007), 222–233.

Pantaleo, Sylvia and Lawrence R. Sipe. 'Introduction: postmodernism and picturebooks.' In *Postmodern Picturebooks: Play, Parody and Self-Referentiality.* Edited by Lawrence R. Sipe and Sylvia Pantaleo, 9–21. New York: Routledge, 2008.

Parsons, Marnie. *Touch Monkeys: Nonsense Strategies for Reading Twentieth Century Poetry.* Toronto: University of Toronto Press, 1994.

Piaget, Jean. *Play, Dreams and Imitation in Childhood.* Translated by C. Gattegno and F. M. Hodgson. New York: W. W. Norton and Co., 1962.

Reece, Lesley. 'Picture book learning and teaching strategy.' The Literature Centre, Fremantle, Western Australia, 2001.

Richards, Janet C. and Nancy A. Anderson. 'What do I *see*? What do I *think*? What do I *wonder*? (STW): A visual literacy strategy to help emergent readers focus on storybook illustrations.' *The Reading Teacher* 56(3) (2003), 442–444.

Rommetveit, Ragnar. 'Language acquisition as increasing linguistic structuring of experience and symbolic behaviour control.' In *Culture, Communication and Cognition: Vygotskian Perspectives.* Edited by James V. Wertsch, 183–204. Cambridge: Cambridge University Press, 1985.

Rosenblatt, Louise M. *The Reader, the Text, the Poem: The Transactional Theory of the Literary Work.* Carbondale and Edwardsville: Southern Illinois University Press, 1978.

Sanches, Mary and Barbara Kirshenblatt-Gimblett. 'Children's traditional speech play and child language.' In *Speech Play: Research and Resources for Studying Linguistic Creativity.* Edited by Barbara Kirshenblatt-Gimblett, 65–110. Philadelphia: University of Pennsylvania Press, 1976.

Scott, A. O. 'Sense and nonsense,' *New York Times Magazine,* 26 November 2000.

Serafini, Frank. '*Voices in the Park,* voices in the classroom: Readers responding to postmodern picture books.' *Reading Research and Instruction* 44(3) (2005), 47–64.

Sidman, Joyce. '*Meow Ruff*: how this book began ...' Retrieved on 28 June 2014 from www.joycesidman.com/books.

Singer, J. L. and D. Singer. *The House of Make Believe*. Cambridge, MA: Cambridge University Press, 1990.

Sipe, Lawrence R. 'First graders interpret David Wiesner's *The Three Pigs*: a case study.' In *Postmodern Picturebooks: Play, Parody and Self-Referentiality*. Edited by Lawrence R. Sipe and Sylvia Pantaleo, 223–237. New York: Routledge, 2008.

Snow, Catherine E. 'The development of conversation between mothers and babies.' In *Child Language: A Reader*. Edited by Margery B. Franklin and Sybil B. Barten, 20–35. Oxford: Oxford University Press, 1988.

Stephens, John. *Language and Ideology in Children's Fiction*. London: Longman, 1992.

Stephens, John. '"They are always surprised at what people throw away": glocal postmodernism in Australian picturebooks.' In *Postmodern Picturebooks: Play, Parody and Self-Referentiality*. Edited by Lawrence R. Sipe and Sylvia Pantaleo, 89–102. New York: Routledge, 2008.

Stephens, John, Ken Watson and Judith Parker. *From Picture Book to Literary Theory*. Sydney: St Clair Press, 2003.

Stewart, Susan. *Nonsense: Aspects of Intertextuality in Folklore and Literature*. Baltimore, MD: Johns Hopkins University Press, 1978.

Sutton-Smith, Brian. 'Epilogue: play as performance.' In *Play and Learning*. Edited by Brian Sutton-Smith, 295–322. New York: Gardner Press, 1979.

Sutton-Smith, Brian. *The Ambiguity of Play*. Cambridge, MA: Harvard University Press, 1997.

Tan, Shaun. '*The Lost Thing*.' Retrieved on 28 June 2014 from www.shauntan.net/books.html.

TeachingBooks.net. 'Anthony Browne.' Interview retrieved on 28 June 2014 from www.teachingbooks.net/content/Browne_qu.pdf.

Thibault, Melissa. 'Reading picture books.' Retrieved on 28 June 2014 from www.learnnc.org/lp/pages/669.

Tigges, Wim. 'An anatomy of literary nonsense.' In *Explorations in the Field of Nonsense*. Edited by Wim Tigges, 23–46. Amsterdam: Rodopi, 1987.

Trevarthen, C. 'Sharing making sense: intersubjectivity and the making of an infant's meaning.' In *Language Topics: Essays in Honour of Michael Halliday*. Edited by R. Steele and T. Threadgold, vol. 1, 177–199. Amsterdam: John Benjamins, 1987.

Trevarthen, C. 'The self born in intersubjectivity: the psychology of an infant communicating.' In *The Perceived Self: Ecological and Interpersonal Sources of Self-Knowledge*. Edited by Ulric Neisser, 121–173. Cambridge: Cambridge University Press, 1993.

Trevarthen, C. and P. Hubley. 'Secondary intersubjectivity: confidence, confiding, and acts of meaning in the first year.' In *Action, Gesture, and Symbol*. Edited by A. Lock, 183–229. London: Academic Press, 1978.

UK Chartered Institute of Library and Information Professionals (CILIP). *Kate Greenaway Visual Literacy Project*. Retrieved on 28 June 2014 from www.carnegiegreenaway.org.uk/celebration/reading_resources.php#reader_development_pack_2.

Vygotsky, L. S. *Mind in Society: The Development of Higher Psychological Processes*. Edited by M. Cole, V. John-Steiner, S. Scribner and E. Souberman. Cambridge, MA: Harvard University Press, 1978.

Warner, Marina. *No Go the Bogeyman: Scaring, Lulling and Making Mock*. London: Chatto and Windus, 1998.

Watkins, Tony and Zena Sutherland. 'Contemporary children's literature (1970–present).' In *Children's Literature: An Illustrated History*. Edited by Peter Hunt, 289–321. Oxford: Oxford University Press, 1995.

Watson, Ken. 'The postmodern picture book in the secondary classroom.' *English in Australia* 140 (2004), 55–57.

Waugh, Patricia. *Metafiction: The Theory and Practice of Self-Conscious Fiction*. London: Methuen, 1984.

Wellman, H. M. *The Child's Theory of Mind*. Cambridge, MA: Bradford/MIT Press, 1990.

Wiesner, David. 'What is *flotsam*?' Retrieved on 28 June 2014 from www.thefishknowthesecret.com/logs.

Wiesner, David. 'Say, what? *Mr Wuffles!*' Retrieved on 28 June 2014 from www.davidwiesner.com/work/say-what.

Williams, Geoffrey. 'Children entering literate worlds: perspectives from the study of textual practices.' In *Literacy and Schooling*. Edited by Frances Christie and Ray Misson, 18–46. London: Routledge, 1998.

Williams, Geoffrey and David Jack. 'The role of story: learning to read in a special education class.' In *Revaluing Troubled Readers*, Occasional Paper no. 15, 12–39. Tucson, AZ: Program in Language and Literacy, University of Arizona, 1986.

Winnicott, D. W. *Playing and Reality*. London: Routledge, 1971.

Wolf, Shelby Anne and Shirley Brice Heath. *The Braid of Literature: Children's Worlds of Reading*. Cambridge, MA: Harvard University Press, 1992.

Index

CPSIA information can be obtained at www.ICGtesting.com
Printed in the USA
BVOW06*1825150316

440438BV00003B/9/P